CULTURES OF THE WORLD

Latvia

Robert Barlas and Winnie Wong

Marshall Cavendish
Benchmark
New York

PICTURE CREDITS

Cover: © Niall Benvie/CORBIS
Anne-Christine Poujoulat/AFP/Getty Images: 95 • Audrius Tomonis: 135 • David Rubinger/Time Life Pictures/ Getty Images:42 • Dimitar Dilkoff/AFP/Getty Images: 30 • Francis Tan: 130, 131 • Haga Library Japan: 14, 53, 56, 61, 83, 96, 111, 112, 113, 114, 116, 124, 126, 129 • Hutchison Library: 8, 43 • Ilmars Znotins/AFP/Getty Images: 31, 34, 35, 37, 38, 39, 47, 49, 62, 67, 97 • Janek Skarzynski/AFP/Getty Images: 65 • Michael Steele/ Getty Images for UCI: 109 • North Wind Picture Archive: 20 • photolibrary: 2, 5, 6, 9, 10, 12, 13, 15, 17, 17, 18, 24, 25, 26, 27, 28, 32, 33, 40, 41, 45, 46, 48, 50, 52, 55, 64, 68, 72, 76, 78, 79, 81, 82, 86, 89, 90, 92, 98, 100, 104, 110, 120, 121, 122, 125, 128 • Tom Cockrem/ Lonely Planet Images: 1 • Topham Picturepoint: 11 • Trip Photographic Library: 7, 19, 21, 44, 54, 57, 59, 66, 69, 70, 71, 73, 75, 77, 84, 87, 88, 91, 93, 94, 101, 103, 105, 106, 107, 115, 117, 123, 127 • Universal Images Group/ Getty Images: 51

PRECEDING PAGE
A busker playing the accordian.

Publisher (U.S.): Michelle Bisson
Editors: Deborah Grahame, Stephanie Pee
Copyreader: Tara Tomczyk
Designers: Nancy Sabato, Lock Hong Liang
Cover picture researcher: Connie Gardner
Picture researcher: Thomas Khoo

Marshall Cavendish Benchmark
99 White Plains Road
Tarrytown, NY 10591
Website. www.marshallcavendish.us

Originated and designed by Times Media Private Limited
An imprint of Marshall Cavendish International (Asia) Private Limited
A member of Times Publishing Limited

Marshall Cavendish is a trademark of Times Publishing Limited.

All Internet sites were correct and accurate at the time of printing. All monetary figures in this publication are in U.S. dollars.

Library of Congress Cataloging-in-Publication Data
Barlas, Robert.
  Latvia / Robert Barlas and Winnie Wong. — 2nd ed.
      p. cm. — (Cultures of the world)
  Summary: "Provides comprehensive information on the geography, history, wildlife, governmental structure, economy, cultural diversity, peoples, religion, and culture of Latvia"—Provided by publisher.
  Includes bibliographical references and index.
  ISBN 978-0-7614-4857-0
  1. Latvia—Juvenile literature. I. Wong, Winnie. II. Title.
  DK504.56.B37 2010
  947.96—dc22   2009046001

Printed in China
9 8 7 6 5 4 3 2 1

CONTENTS

>INTRODUCTION

L **ATVIA IS A BALTIC COUNTRY THAT HAS PRESERVED ITS ANCIENT** language, culture, and worldview despite five centuries of invasion and occupation by neighboring powers. Germany, Poland, Sweden, and Russia have all left their marks in the history of Latvia. The Latvians have survived two world wars and fifty years behind the Iron Curtain. Loss of both territory and manpower has not dampened the spirit of its people. Latvia is known as "a nation that sings." Tens of thousands of Latvians regularly gather to sing their *daina* or folk songs, a tradition and symbol that has shaped Latvia's national awakening for two hundred years.

As Latvia completes its second decade of renewed independence, it is even more committed to principles of democracy and international cooperation. Today Latvians have a renewed desire to build their lives in a natural environment and flourish in the arts, education, and economy in a European setting.

GEOGRAPHY

A field of flowers in the Kurzeme region.

CHAPTER 1

LATVIA IS LOCATED IN EASTERN Europe. The country covers an area of 24,931 square miles (64,589 square kilometers), which is slightly larger than the state of West Virginia, or the combined territories of Belgium and the Netherlands in Europe.

Latvia lies across the Baltic Sea from Sweden; south of Finland and Estonia; north of Poland, Lithuania, and Belarus; and west of Russia. Its western boundary runs along the shores of the Baltic Sea and the Gulf of Riga.

Latvia is situated on the northern edge of the European Plain, a relatively flat landscape with gently rolling hills. The characteristics of the land were formed during the Ice Age when large masses of ice moved across the area. The Baltic Sea coast of Latvia consists of a coastal plain of 308 miles (496 km) long. The flatness of this area, a former sea bottom, is occasionally broken by coastal ridges, but plains are the predominant landform throughout the country.

REGIONS

Latvia is divided into five major regions—Zemgale, Kurzeme, Vidzeme, Latgale, and the capital area of Riga.

Right: Harvest time on a farm outside Riga.

Latvia is a low lying country in eastern Europe. It is home to almost 3,000 lakes and is watered by four major rivers.

The region of Zemgale is bisected by the Zemgale Plain and is dominated by the Lielupe River. The plain is a depository of sandy clay and is the most fertile grain-producing area of the country. Hilly areas can be found to the west and in the southeastern part of the region, especially at its borders with the Daugava, Latvia's principal river.

To the west, the region of Kurzeme is more undulating than Zemgale. The hills of Vidzeme to the northeast and Latgale to the east are interspersed with lowland areas, river valleys, lakes, marshes, and boglands. The soil of Vidzeme and Latgale is poorer and less suited to crop farming than the soil in Zemgale and Kurzeme. Latgale is crisscrossed by streams and interconnected by lakes with numerous islets, and it is often referred to as Latvia's lake district.

LAKES AND MOUNTAINS

Latvia is a very low country. The average elevation is only 285 feet (87 meters) above sea level, whereas its highest point, called Gaiziņš, located in the uplands of central Vidzeme, is only 1,024 feet (312 m).

Rivers, lakes, and harbors play an important role in the cultural and national identity of the Latvians. Bodies of water are the subject of many Latvian legends and folk songs, which refer to their origins and beauty and to events that occurred on them.

A Latvian man fishing in the floodplain of a river after heavy rains.

There are about 2,250 lakes in Latvia. The largest is Lake Lubans, covering an area of 31.1 square miles (80.7 square km). The deepest is Lake Dridzis at 214 feet (65.1 m). Both lakes are located in the Latgale region in the east.

RIVERS

The four major rivers in Latvia are the Daugava, Lielupe, Venta, and Gauja, but there are numerous small rivers and streams, some 12,000 in all, but only 17 are longer than 60 miles (97 km).

The Daugava, which begins in central Russia, is the largest river, flowing through Belarus before entering Latvia to empty into the Gulf of Riga. The total length of the Daugava is 624 miles (1,005 km).

The Venta originates in Lithuania. It is renowned for its waterfall, called the Rumba, at the city of Kuldīga. The river mouth forms a natural harbor for oceangoing ships at Ventspils, where it flows into the Baltic Sea.

Autumn trees along the Gajua River.

Turaida Castle covered in snow.

CLIMATE AND SEASONS

Despite being situated quite far north, Latvia's climate is relatively temperate, with mild winters and moderately warm summers. Spring comes in late March when flooding is common, due to melting snow and the break up of river ice. The mild, warm summer weather arrives in June and lasts until September. This is the season of the heaviest rainfall, with frequent thunderstorms and precipitation. Typically July is the warmest month of the year, with an average temperature of 60.44°F (15.8°C).

During the fall months, there is frost, high humidity, and fog, particularly in coastal areas. Winter sets in around November. January is the coldest month, with an average temperature of 23.9°F (-4.5°C). Most snowfall occurs between January and March. Despite the small size of the country, there are marked differences in climate from west to east in Latvia.

FLORA AND FAUNA

There are three main plant habitats in Latvia—coniferous and broadleaf forests, swampy marshes, and grass-covered meadows. Forests, more than half of which are pinewood, cover approximately 42 percent of the country.

In Latvia there are about 18,047 different animal species, including rodents, such as squirrels and beavers, and carnivores such as wolves, foxes, lynx, and martens. Many of Latvia's animals can also be found in other countries in the region—wild boar, elk, red deer, and the swamp turtle.

The American mink and the Norwegian rat have been accidentally introduced into Latvia. Other nonnative animals include the jenot (a kind of raccoon), fallow deer, and wild rabbits.

There are more than 344 species of birds in Latvia. These include the storks, the common water fowl, turtle and rock doves, several species of grouse, the barn owl, the house swallow, the greenish warbler, and even the Arctic loon. The white wagtail is the national bird of Latvia.

Elk grazing. Before the beginning of farming, forests covered about 80 percent of the land.

Latvians welcome storks, believing they bring good fortune to the family, not just babies. Almost at every third farmhouse, a pair of white storks can be found nesting. Endangered black storks nest in secluded parts of old forests. About 10 percent of the world's black storks are found in Latvia. They are an important pollution indicator for the environment.

MAJOR CITIES

Most of Latvia's present-day urban centers evolved from early settlements near rivers and other sites along trade routes. The cities developed their own local traditions, religious character, and political systems, which were tempered over the years by the various occupying powers—Poland, Sweden, Germany, and Russia. The major cities in Latvia today are Ventspils, Riga, Daugavpils, Liepaja, Jelgava, Jurmala, and Rezekne.

RIGA   Riga is the capital of Latvia. It is situated on the Daugava River estuary, where it flows into the Baltic Sea.

Riga was an important trading post during the Viking Age. It was officially established as a city by the German Sword Brothers, who built fortresses along the river. The Citadel of Riga was built in the 17th century, and Riga soon became one of the strongest fortresses and shipping ports on the eastern coast of the Baltic Sea.

The Daugava River and railroad bridge in Riga.

During the 1930s Riga was referred to as "the Paris of the north," with its grand streets and broad boulevards. The old historic part of the city, known as the Old Town (or Vecrīga), has been preserved and protected over the centuries, and most of the area has been restored to its original state with narrow cobblestone streets, richly decorated doors, tile roofs, and churches.

The focal point of the modern city of Riga is the Liberty Monument, where Latvians gather to show their love and devotion to their homeland and to remember the despair and hope of the long years of the Soviet occupation.

DAUGAVPILS Daugavpils, the second-largest city in Latvia, is situated in the southeast on the Daugava River. The first written record of Daugavpils is from 1275, but archaeological digs show that the area has been inhabited since the Stone Age. Daugavpils is the administrative center of the Latgale region and is an important transportation junction in eastern Latvia. Due to its proximity to Russia, Belarus, and Lithuania, Daugavpils has become an important center of trade and commerce.

An aerial view of the city of Riga.

Daugavpils is also noted for its rich and varied cultural and educational activities. Russian, Belarusian, Jewish, Lithuanian, Polish, and many other societies do their best to preserve and support their own traditions. The Daugavpils Pedagogical University is noted as a national training center for teachers, while scientists from Latvia and abroad study at the Latgale Research Institute.

LIEPĀJA Liepāja is located on Lake Liepāja, where its waters enter the Baltic Sea. It has a population of 86,000 and has been inhabited since the ninth century. Liepāja has been part of many different countries since 1625, including Sweden, Prussia, the Russian Empire, and the former Soviet Union.

One of the city's major features is its artificial harbor, which was built between 1697 and 1703. It was deepened in the middle of the 19th century

Many of the old buildings in the older sections of Latvian cities have been restored to their former glory following independence.

to remain ice-free during the cold winter months. As a gateway to the West the entry became an important communications center in 1869 when it was linked with Copenhagen by an undersea cable.

During the Soviet occupation, access to Liepāja was restricted because of the large Russian naval base there. Liepāja is noted for its excellent port facilities, as well as being an important Latvian industrial center.

JELGAVA Jelgava is situated on the banks of the Lielupe River, which serves as a major transportation route between Riga and Lithuania. It was officially founded in 1573 but was mentioned in historic documents dating back to 1265.

As the capital of the Zemgale region, Jelgava first developed as an active trade and commerce center. During the 18th century it was also a

Liepāja city in Latvia.

printing center. The first Latvian newspaper, *Latviešu Avīzes*, was printed here and elsewhere, as were half of all Latvian language books. Today, industrial activity in Jelgava includes metallurgy, engineering, textiles, plastics, woodworking, and publishing. Jelgava also has a research center for forest and wood products as well as construction materials. Jelgava's most important landmark is the 300-room, Baroque-style Jelgava Castle, which was designed by Italian architect F. B. Rastrelli. It took over 30 years to complete. It is located on the site of a castle built by the Livonian Order in 1265, near the Lielupe River. The original castle was destroyed during World War I, but it was rebuilt during Latvia's first period of independence.

VENTSPILS Ventspils is located on the shores of the Baltic Sea at the mouth of the Venta River in western Latvia. The city was an important trade and commercial center throughout its history, and the mouth of the Venta was known to navigators as early as the 12th century. In early times it

In 2002 Ventspils was the first Eastern European city to host the international Cow Parade exhibition and auction event. Artists painted and displayed life-size fiberglass cow sculptures to raise money for charity.

Miatu Castle in Jelgava.

was inhabited by the Couronian (or Kurs), then by the Livonian Order in the 13th century.

Ventspils became a shipbuilding center during and after the Duchy of Courland. During the 17th century it was an important port of the Duchy of Courland, which included Kurzeme and Zemgale provinces. The city continues to be a major transportation center. The main activity of the port is transshipment of oil, potassium, and forest products, and the city has a number of gas and oil refineries and chemical manufacturing facilities. Its world-class port is ice-free, and the world's largest tanker and cargo ship can be docked in its deepened shipping canal all year round.

Today major ecological cleanup efforts to repair the damage caused from extensive environmental neglect during the Soviet era has successfully transformed Ventspils into a tourist destination.

A building in Ventspils.

HISTORY

Freedom Monument in Riga, built to celebrate
total liberation from Russia.

CHAPTER 2

T HE FIRST INHABITANTS OF LATVIA were nomadic tribes who migrated along the Baltic Sea after the last Ice Age some 10,000 years ago. In 2000 B.C., a new group of settlers—the proto-Balts or early Baltic people—came from the south and established permanent settlements on the eastern shore of the Baltic Sea in the territory known today as Latvia.

The Finnic people—early ancestors of the Estonians, Finns, and Livonians—were already in these lands before the arrival of the Balts.

Between the second and fifth centuries A.D., Baltic tribes traded the semiprecious stone, amber, and the link between the Baltic countries and those on the Mediterranean Sea became known as the Amber Route.

Latvia was constantly occupied by other European powers, namely Germany and Russia. Power over Latvia frequently changed hands. By 1795 Russia regained control over Latvia. Only in 1918 did Latvia finally declare independence, although fighting continued. A peace treaty with the Soviet Union was signed in 1920, in which Latvia's sovereignty was recognized.

Ivan the Terrible being rebuked by a church official. His reign was productive until he became ill in 1553. He used scorched-earth tactics to advance to Latvia, leaving total destruction in the wake of his army.

Latvia became famous for its amber, and a trading network was established from Scandinavia along the Daugava River, and a trade route to Constantinople and Persia was established as well.

Around A.D. 900, the Balts began to establish individual tribal cultures—Couronians, Semigallians, Selonians, and Letgallians.

In the 1100s and 1200s, the Couronians, who had settled along the west coast of the Baltic became known as the "Baltic Vikings" who—similar to the Scandinavian Vikings —traveled far to raid and loot, as well as trade. The other inland tribes were peace-loving farmers.

The Germans were the first to succeed in invading Latvia. The first German merchants arrived in the second half of the 12th century. In 1198 Pope Innocent II proclaimed the Baltic Crusade. His aim was to cut off the northern trade routes of Constantinople as well as convert the people of the Baltic region to Roman Catholicism. The crusade ended a century later, when the last Latvian tribe was subjugated. Riga was founded by the Germanic Bishop Albert I of Livonia in 1201, and within a hundred years it joined the Hansa League, forming important cultural and economic relationships with all countries of Europe.

THE DUCHY OF COURLAND

In 1237 the Latvians, including tribes in what is now known as Estonia, were under complete German domination, and the area was united by the Teutonic Knights into a state known as the Confederation of Livonia. For the next 270 years, Latvians gradually turned into serfs under these German-speaking knights, merchants, and church officials.

The local German nobility, who were landowners, requested protection from Poland during the Livonian War from 1558 to 1583 when Ivan the Terrible of Russia invaded Latvia. The Muscovites (as the Russians were called at that time) were not completely successful in conquering Livonia, as they faced opposition from the Poles. Ivan's armies were eventually driven out. In return the greater part of Latvia was incorporated into the Kingdom of Poland, while the western part of Latvia became an autonomous Duchy of Courland under Poland's protection.

For the next 200 years, the Duchy of Courland remained an independent naval and commercial power in Northern Europe with its own army, navy, and, until 1795, its own monetary system.

FOREIGN DOMINATION

Latvia continued to be a political football for many years. During the Polish-Swedish War from 1600 to 1629, Sweden acquired the region of Vidzeme and

The demands made of the Latvian peasants during Russian domination forced them further into debt.

Riga. The Swedish king, Gustav II, brought about immediate administrative and judicial reforms and made great efforts to strengthen Lutheranism and foster education. Taxation was based on the amount of property a person owned. Land surveys and censuses produced the first detailed maps of Latvia. Schools and courts were established for the native population. Historians often refer to this period as the "good old Swedish Era." However, local nobility resisted these Swedish reforms and kept most of the ethnic Latvian population as serfs.

The Swedes ruled Vidzeme and Riga until 1710. Riga, the largest city in Sweden's empire, was an important link to major states and cultures of Western, Eastern, and Northern Europe. Vidzeme supplied the Swedish kingdom with wheat and is known as "Sweden's bread basket."

During the Great Northern War, the Russians first defeated Sweden from 1700 to 1710 and expanded its borders into Vidzeme and Riga. Later, between 1778 and 1795, Russia annexed eastern Poland and brought Latgale, Zemgale, and Kurzeme under Russian control. The Swedish judicial reforms were thrown out, and the conditions of Latvian peasants deteriorated once more. Their compulsory labor was increased to six days a week, while the landed gentries were exempt from taxation. During this period many beautiful castles were built on the estates of the Baltic barons. To support their lavish lifestyle, landlords demanded higher taxes from the peasants.

The economic and social domination of the Latvian people reached its lowest point during Polish and Russian domination. Landlords acquired more and more land and forced excessive taxes on the peasants.

NATIONAL AWAKENING BEGINS

The Age of Enlightenment, a period when a belief developed in the power of reason, science, and the possibility of human change for the better, spread through Europe in the 18th century, but was slow in coming to Latvia. Although a tract advocating the complete emancipation of the peasants was published in the late 1700s, the ethnic German gentries strongly opposed any reforms and were powerful enough to resist change for a long time. Beginning in

RISE OF NATIONALISM

The most prominent leaders of the first National Awakening Movement (1850—70) were Krišjānis Barons, a leading scholar of folk poetry, and Krišjānis Valdemars, who established a maritime school of navigation and shipping business. Juris Alunāns was the first widely published poet, and later, Atis Kronvalds became a fiery orator who criticized German domination of social and economic life in Latvia. Kārlis Baumanis was the organizer of the first National Song Festival (1873) and author of the national anthem of Latvia. These poets and writers modernized the Latvian language, making it suitable for literature as well as contemporary science and business. When government censorship was relaxed, they published the first Latvian-language newspapers. They fought to establish schools for the non-German population. In Riga, Latvians established numerous cultural organizations, such as the National Song Festival, which brings together choirs from all over the Latvian-speaking territory.

1818, a series of laws were passed in which the peasants were given personal freedom and limited freedom of movement. Some Latvians succeeded in getting basic schooling for their children. However, most Latvians were still dependent on their landlords for their livelihood. A major breakthrough came in 1868 when a law was passed to eliminate mandatory service to manors. This forced the gentry to hire labor and to sell an ever-increasing amount of land to their former tenants to obtain cash.

RUSSIFICATION

As a result of finally being able to buy their own land, a much larger number of Latvians became landowners in the latter part of the 19th century and so began to have the financial resources to educate their children and take part in social and cultural activities. The University of Tartu was the nearest institution of higher education, and by the 1850s it was attracting significant numbers of Latvian students. With this growth of education, Latvians became reacquainted with their history and their ethnic heritage, which led in turn to a growth in national identity.

Walter Zapp (1905–2003) invented and produced the first Minox miniature camera in 1938. A number of these cameras were used by espionage agencies in several countries during World War II.

Russian soldiers in action near Riga.

Ironically, soon after this reawakening of national feeling, Latvia was undergoing a major wave of Russification—Russians only in all official positions, the Russian language mandatory in schools and in all institutions, and enforcement of the Russian Orthodox faith. The revolution of 1905 in Russia was a turning point that inspired the Latvians to take up arms against their German landlords and Russian rulers. Although this revolt was put down mercilessly by czarist troops, the stage was set for Latvia's war of independence 13 years later.

INDEPENDENCE

On November 18, 1918, Latvians declared national independence and formed a provisional government. The war of independence had begun. Fighting continued for the next two years against the leftist social democrats known as the Bolsheviks in Russia, who—despite leader Valdimir Lenin's promises—wanted to incorporate Latvia into the new Soviet Russia, and also against the Germans, who had similar plans for Latvia.

By 1920 the Germans and the Bolsheviks were both defeated by the Latvian national armed forces. Latvia signed a peace treaty with the Soviets in which the Soviet Union recognized "unconditionally the independence and sovereignty of Latvia and declines, voluntary and for all times, all claims on the Latvian people and territory which formerly belonged to Russia." Latvia was established as a democratic republic, and the first period of Latvia's real political independence began.

Latvia's democratic, parliamentary government was recognized by all the world powers. On September 22, 1921, an independent Latvia was admitted to the League of Nations.

Prisoners from the concentration camp at Salaspils were liberated in 1944 by the Red Army.

Latvia's democratic government was briefly interrupted from 1934 to 1940 in an authoritarian coup led by prime minister Kārlis Ulmanis. He dissolved the Saeima (parliament) and established executive non-parliamentary authoritarian rule. Key government offices, communications and transportation facilities were removed. The incumbent president Alberts Kviesis served out the rest of his term until 1936, after which Ulmanis merged the office of president and prime minister. When the Soviets reoccupied Latvia in 1940, Ulmanis was forced to resign.

A NEW ECONOMY

Following independence, laws were passed concerning the redistribution of land, and the number of landowning farmers increased by nearly 100 percent. Several hundred ethnic German families had owned more than half of the farmlands in Latvia. These were taken back and redistributed to volunteers in Latvia's war for independence. The first decade of independence also saw

The Monument for Liberators in Jelgava bears testament to the struggle Latvia endured during its long fight for independence.

the rebuilding of the economy. Farming shifted from grain to dairy production, and food exports became a stable source of national income. Most factory equipment had been evacuated to Russia during World War I, and never returned. New factories were established to produce consumer goods. Forest products were also profitable exports. The State Electrotechnical Factory began to produce radios and telephone equipment. A hydroelectric generating station supplied 40 percent of Latvia's electric power.

MOLOTOV-RIBBENTROP PACT

But Latvia's independence did not last. In 1939 the Soviet Union and Nazi Germany signed the Molotov-Ribbentrop Pact, which included a secret protocol that consigned independent Latvia, along with Estonia and Finland, to the Soviet sphere of influence.

In October 1939 Latvia received an ultimatum from Moscow demanding the immediate free entry of Soviet troops into Latvia's territory. The Red Army crossed the Latvian border on the following day, and in June 1940 a Soviet-installed government took power. During the next 12 months, more than 32,000 people were deported or executed, and entire families were sent to labor camps in Siberia. About 20,000 Latvian men were drafted into the Red Army.

SOVIET LATVIA

Soviet subjugation of Latvia was interrupted by the beginning of the German-Soviet War. By 1941 the German Nazis had occupied all of Latvia, exacting their own terror on the populace. About 70,000 Latvian Jews (nearly the entire Jewish population), were brutally murdered between August and November that year. Their bodies were buried in mass graves such as the one near Rumbula. About 18,000 Latvians also perished. Initially Latvians hoped that the Germans would reinstate Latvia's independence, but this did not happen. Konstantins Cakste, head of the underground Latvian government, was arrested and deported to Germany, where he died in prison.

In the following years, Nazi Germany began to suffer regular defeats when fighting Soviet troops on the eastern front. From 1944 to 1945 Latvia was once again reoccupied by the Soviet Union. This time Russian dominance would last for nearly 50 years and bring with it new waves of terror and deportations. Armed resistance against the Russian occupation lasted until 1956 when it was finally crushed, and all symbols of Latvia's independence were outlawed or altered. Russian was imposed as the official language, farms owners and their families were deported, and their properties were taken over by the government. Factories, too, were now owned by the state. Moreover, a large number of Russians, Ukrainians, and Belarusians were moved to Latvia between 1944 and 1991. In 1959, the Latvian communist government led by Eduards Berklavs attempted to slow the immigration of Russians into Latvia. He was quickly removed from power and relocated to Russia, while many other Latvians, communist and noncommunist alike, lost their jobs and were persecuted by the Soviet government. People lost their rights to freedom of speech, freedom of assembly, and freedom of religious worship. Even owning a banned book or distributing a handwritten political statement were sufficient reasons for arrest and imprisonment in a labor camp.

The Latgale Liberation Monument commemorates the freedom fighters' struggle to escape foreign domination.

For the next 50 years, the seat of government and the real power was in Moscow, and Latvia was subjected to a totalitarian way of life where power belonged entirely to the Communist Party of the Soviet Union. Private ownership was prohibited. The state controlled every aspect of an individual's life—from cradle to grave.

Children attended state-run kindergartens and state-run schools later on. They had to join the Young Pioneers—a state-run organization for young people where control could be maintained over the activities of members and where ongoing political and social indoctrination could be conducted. Later, if they wished to study at a university, they would have to join the Communist Youth Organization (Komsomol).

COLLECTIVE FARMS

With private property abolished, most city inhabitants were forced to live in apartments that belonged to the state. These tended to be small and

A reconstruction of a farmhouse.

cramped with several separate families living in one apartment, sharing a kitchen and bathroom. The rent was set at a fixed rate, but the government had the power to raise it at its will.

In the countryside, family farms were liquidated and replaced by state-controlled collective farms. If a farm was larger than 20 acres, its owner and his family were classified as "kulaks," or prosperous. More than 10,000 of these people, about half of them children, were deported to Siberia. Pride in work and in one's surroundings disappeared as personal freedom of movement was curtailed. Civil liberties ceased to exist, and arrests, interrogations, and deportations were common.

ISOLATION FROM THE WEST

By the 1960s the Soviet Union and the countries allied with it were absolutely cut off from the outside world. This means no communication existed with the West, and news from other parts of the world was not available, except when it suited the government.

The desire of the populace to regain independence was silenced by the state rule of the Communist Party and the KGB, its intelligence and internal security agency. Moreover, religious and human rights activists were routinely arrested and consigned to prison camps in the Soviet Union. Until the late 1980s, the campaign for Latvia's independence in the international political arena was mostly carried on by the over 120,000 Latvian exiles in the West who had fled the country in 1944 and 1945. They maintained contacts with dissidents in Latvia and publicized their activities in the world media.

LATVIA TODAY

Latvia's third National Awakening began with a demonstration in 1987 in defiance of local authorities. It was held at the Liberty Monument in Riga to commemorate the victims of the 1941 Soviet deportation. After this, with each subsequent rally and demonstration, the old rules established

Latvia's independence movement, called the "Singing Revolution," rejected violence as a political weapon, achieving independence in 1991.

by the Soviet regime began to fall. Even the communist government of Soviet Latvia joined the movement, declaring Latvian to be the official language of the republic, and reinstating the national flag after a mammoth demonstration of 300,000 people in July 1988. On August 23, 1989, after 50 years of the Molotov-Ribbentrop Pact, nonformal organizations sprang up everywhere, uniting to form a single political organization, the Popular Front (Tautas Fronte). The Popular Front joined similar organizations in Estonia and Lithuania to organize the largest-ever Baltic demonstration—the "Baltic Way." A 373-mile-long (600-km-long) human chain, made up of more than a million people from the three Baltic states—Estonia, Latvia, and Lithuania—stretched from Tallinn in Estonia, through Riga to Vilnius in Lithuania.

In 1990, for the first time ever under Soviet rule, voters had a choice of two political groups: the Communist Party, which favored remaining in the Soviet Union, and the Popular Front, which desired independence.

A woman places flowers at the foot of the Liberty Monument, marking Latvia's Day of Independence.

The Popular Front won two-thirds of the vote, and on May 4, 1990, the newly elected parliament voted to restore Latvia's prewar status as an independent republic with a transitional period. During the crackdown on Lithuanian and Latvian independence in January 1991, Soviet OMON (*Otryad Militsii Osobogo Naznacheniya*, a special purpose police unit) troops killed five people in Riga. But by August 21, after the collapse of a coup in Moscow, Latvia succeeded in the complete reinstatement of its independence. After a constitutional convention that renewed the democratic system established in 1918, the first free parliamentary elections were held in 1993. The prewar currency, the Latvian lat, again became the official currency. In 1994 Latvian President Guntis Ulmanis and his Russian counterpart, Boris Yeltsin, signed an agreement to withdraw all Russian troops from Latvian soil. Following the renewed independence, Latvia quickly returned to the international milieu. It became a member of the Organization for Security and Co-operation in Europe (OSCE) and the United Nations (UN) in 1991. In 1998, Latvia began negotiations to join the European Union (EU) and the North Atlantic Treaty Organization (NATO), and became a member of both in 2004. Its pro-market, pro—free trade policies enabled Latvia to become EU's fastest-growing economy from 2004 through 2006.

Pensioners in Latvia protesting against cutting pensions in a bid to reduce the country's budget deficit.

The world economic crisis in 2008 caused Latvia's economy to collapse. Output fell more than 10 percent in the last quarter that year and many people found themselves without work. Public anger spilled into the streets in January 2009 as scores of protesters clashed with police when they tried to storm the parliament. More than forty people were injured in Latvia's worst riots since the country gained independence from the Soviet Union.

GOVERNMENT

Tower of the Riga Castle, the seat of the
Latvian government and residence of the
Latvian president.

LATVIA IS AN INDEPENDENT democratic republic. The constitution provides for separation of legislative, executive, and judicial powers; for the separation of church and state; for freedom of the press, conscience, speech, and assembly; and for equal rights for all citizens, including cultural autonomy for ethnic minorities.

The major political parties in the Saeima, or parliament, include the People's Party (*Tautas Partija*), Union of Greens and Farmers (*Zaļo un*

The town hall in Riga.

Zemnieku Savienība), New Era Party (*Jaunais Laiks*), First Party and Harmony Center (*Saskaņas*) in the 2006 election.

NATIONAL AND LEGAL STRUCTURES

Ultimate power is vested in a single-chamber parliament, the Saeima, which has 100 elected deputies who serve a term of four years. The deputies have control over domestic legislation and international treaties, determine the size of the armed forces, and have veto power over the national budget, which is proposed by the cabinet.

The president is elected by the Saeima for a term of four years for a maximum of two consecutive terms. The president can initiate legislation, appoint diplomatic representatives, and is the commander in chief of the armed forces. He has the power to initiate the dissolution of the Saeima, but the Saeima has the power to dismiss the president by a two-thirds vote.

Latvian president Valdis Zatlers (*right*) with Lithuanian foreign minister Vyaudas Usackas.

The prime minister is proposed by the president, but must be approved by parliament. The prime minister has the power to choose the members of the cabinet, who have voting rights on matters in their areas of responsibility. Latvia's cabinet oversees ministries, such as Social Welfare, Defense, Foreign Affairs, Education and Science, Justice, and Environment.

The judicial structure consists of township courts, justices of the peace, juvenile courts, district courts, a court of appeals, and the supreme court.

CURRENT POLITICAL ISSUES

The main current international political issue is Latvia's commitment to the NATO alliance. Latvia has both military and civilian reconstruction units serving in Afghanistan.

In late 2008 crisis hit Latvia's economy. Less regulation in the banking sector caused Latvia to be affected more deeply than its neighboring

Latvians protesting the government's decision to raise the country's value-added tax (VAT) to 21 percent.

countries. The International Monetary Fund (IMF) and European Union are supporting Latvia with loans. Among the loan conditions is a requirement that Latvia dramatically reduce government spending.

IMMIGRANTS

The issue of acquiring Latvian citizenship through naturalization for foreigners was one of the most difficult matters for the government in the years following independence. In the early 1990s, one-third of the people were not citizens; their ethnicity was mainly Russian (63 percent of all noncitizens), followed by Belarusian (12 percent), and Ukrainian (8 percent). The Latvian government wants to ensure that ethnic Latvian control is maintained but also offers citizenship to the various non-Latvian groups that reside there. To acquire citizenship, a person must have lived in Latvia for five years, must pass a test about the constitution, and pass a basic-level Latvian language examination.

Naturalization increased dramatically when Latvia joined the European Union in 2004. By 2009 about half of the former noncitizens had naturalized, but there were still about 350,000 noncitizen permanent residents of Latvia, or 15 percent of the population. The Latvian government provides ethnic minorities—Russian, Polish, Jewish, Ukrainian, Estonian, Lithuanian, Belarusian, and Roma—with an opportunity to study in their native languages while also learning the Latvian language.

RECENT ELECTIONS

Participation in the political process by the Latvian people declined since the euphoric first years after independence, as a certain level of cynicism developed. There were many political parties, and no distinction among them was clearly visible. Each parliamentary election brought about six to eight parties into parliament, ranging from the nationalist For Fatherland and Freedom to the Russian-speaking Human Rights Party. Government coalitions varied in stability, some lasting several years, others less than a year.

Public impatience for the economic and social benefits of reform was rising, but official corruption was not yet under complete control. Transparency of government decisions was often low, leading to public distrust.

After the 2006 election the new government moved swiftly to remove the head of the Anti-Corruption Bureau, Aleksejs Loskutovs, which led to a mass protest called the "Umbrella Revolution," because it took place on a rainy day. Removal of Loskutovs was temporarily delayed, but was nevertheless completed several months later.

The municipal elections of 2009 resulted in a new shift in Latvian politics. In Riga the winner was the Harmony Party, representing mainly Russian-speaking voters; the new mayor of Riga, Nils Ušakovs, is an ethnic Russian. Harmony chose the First Party, a pro-business, Christian-values party, as its coalition partner.

Latvian voters lining up at a polling station.

LATVIA'S CURRENT LEADERS

Valdis Zatlers, an orthopedic surgeon, won the presidential election and became the seventh president of Latvia in 2007. Zatlers himself is not a member of any political party. He is president of the Latvian Association of Traumatologists and Orthodpaedists, a position he held since 2003. Zatlers participated in the cleanup operations after the disaster at the Chernobyl nuclear plant.

Valdis Dombrovskis was appointed by the parliament as prime minister of Latvia following the resignation of Prime Minister Ivars Godmanis in February 2009. Having lost the support of his two main coalition partners—the People's Party and the Union of Greens and Farmers—and amid protests over the economic crisis, Godmanis stepped down. Dombrovskis, who was minister of finance from 2002 to 2004, had to form a new government to manage the economic decline.

The current prime minister of Latvia, Valdis Dombrovkis.

THE ROLE OF THE MILITARY

Latvia bases its defense concept on four pillars: a collective defense as a member of NATO, professional armed forces, support and coordination with civil society, and international military cooperation.

Currently the national forces of Latvia include the National Armed Forces, Ground Forces, the Navy, Latvian Air Force, Border Guard, and the Latvian Home Guard, called Latvijas Zemessardze.

At the age of 18 young men may volunteer for military service. Since January 2007 conscription to the armed forces had been abolished. Under current law, every Latvian citizen is entitled to serve in the armed forces. The National Armed Forces (NAF) exists to protect Latvia from potential threats to its national security and organized crime. Another involvement of the NAF is participation in international peacekeeping operations.

The Home Guard is under the direct authority of the president. The Security Service consists of a special battalion of soldiers whose job is to fight against terrorists and to provide escorts for visiting dignitaries.

Latvian soldiers march during a military parade celebrating Latvia's 90th year of independence.

ECONOMY

The Hansa Bank headquarters, the Saules Akmens building, along the Daugava River.

CHAPTER 4

H AVING REGAINED INDEPENDENCE in 1991, Latvia inherited the remnants of the state-controlled industries that had been under Soviet control for 50 years. The new leaders had the difficult task of moving the country from a centralized, state-controlled economy to a free market—style economy.

Major industries, which had been totally dependent on raw materials and energy from the former Soviet Union, were privatized, upgraded,

The busy port of Riga is one of the ports in Latvia that supports the country's import and export industries.

After gaining independence, Latvia had the difficult task of rebuilding the economy from a centralized one to a free-market system. Latvia's economy is supported by the service, industry, and agricultural sectors. The recent global recession, however, has set the growth in Latvian economy back. This has resulted in an increase in unemployment.

and restructured to become competitive with those in Western economies. By 1996 more than 93 percent of state-owned enterprises had been privatized through the Latvian Privatization Agency. By the end of the 1990s the private sector produced almost 90 percent of the country's gross domestic product (GDP). Latvia's economy grew more than 10 percent (GDP) during 2006 and 2007, but it experienced a recession in 2008 as a result of a global financial crisis, current account deficit, inflation, and also insufficient banking regulation during the rapid growth of real estate values in the early 21st century.

INDUSTRIES

Latvia's economy is based on services, industry, forest products, and agriculture. Transit trade through three ice-free harbors (Riga, Ventspils, and Liepaja) makes up a significant portion of the service sector. Industries include metalworking; machinery and tools; electrical equipment; textiles and footwear; technological instruments; construction materials; pharmaceuticals; and processed food. The service industry includes

The assembly line at a minibus manufacturing plant.

A lumberjack. Under Latvian law, all workers must be paid at least minimum wage.

retail and wholesale trade, real estate, business activities, transportation, storage, and communication. This sector grossed 74.2 percent of GDP in 2008.

Hydroelectric power is produced in Latvia by three hydroelectric-generating stations located on the Daugava River. Approximately 50 percent of Latvia's electricity supply comes from Estonia, Lithuania, and Russia. Latvia has no oil or natural gas deposits, so gas is imported from Russia. Peat is still used as an energy source and is also exported.

Latvia's chief exports are wood products and agricultural products. Most of Latvia's exports are to other European Union countries.

Imports from European Union countries constitute the largest overall percentage and include machinery and equipment; motor vehicles; mineral and chemical products; food and beverages; and rubber and plastic products.

WORKING LIFE

The employment code approved by the Latvian government in 1992 regulates all employment legislations, and a minimum wage has been set by the law.

The average unemployment rate in Latvia was about 7.5 percent in 2008, but it grew to 19.7 percent in the third quarter of 2009, making it the highest in the European Union.

Every employee maintains a "workbook" documenting his or her work history that is generally submitted to an organization at the time of employment, and the workbook is returned to the employee upon termination of employment. The typical workweek in industry is 40 hours in a five-day week. Vacations may range from two weeks to one month.

REVENUE AND TRADE

With the regaining of independence, Latvia had to introduce its own system of revenue generation. The main sources of revenue are taxes—mainly a social welfare tax in the form of a flat-rate payroll tax. This method of taxation was first introduced by Estonia in 1994 and other Baltic states, including Latvia, were quick to adopt it. In an effort to cut budgets and increase revenue, Latvia's finance ministry plans to replace the flat-rate tax with a progressive tax by 2010. High-wage earners will pay a higher rate of income tax. In 2009 the government also moved to increase revenue by expanding taxes on capital gains and real estate.

The Latvian currency, the lat, was introduced after Latvia gained independence.

TRANSPORTATION

As in many other parts of the world, owning a car is the aim of every Latvian family. As a result the number of cars on the roads is growing at a rapid rate. The European Union has contributed large subsidies to rebuild and improve roads and other infrastructure that declined after decades of neglect during the Soviet period. As Russia's economy booms, routes through Latvia are clogged with trucks bearing new cars, television sets, and machinery. Lines of between 700 and 1,000 trucks regularly wait at the two main crossing points to Russia, and processing can take between 60 and 72 hours.

The number of cars on Latvian roads is increasing.

There are three main seaports that can accommodate oceangoing vessels in Latvia—Ventspils, Riga, and Liepaja. The main activity in these ports is the transshipment of cargo from countries formerly part of the Soviet Union to countries in the West. A regular ferry service from Riga to Stockholm leaves daily from both destination ports. The journey takes about 16 hours each way. A number of small fishing ports dot the coast of the Gulf of Riga.

The airports in Riga, Ventspils, and Liepaja handle local and international passenger and cargo traffic. Trains link Latvia to Germany, Ukraine, Russia, Lithuania, and Estonia. Within Latvia travelling by bus is inexpensive and faster than trains. Riga also has a commuter rail that provides extensive service.

Latvian Railway's international trains travel from Latvia to Lithuania, Estonia, Russia, Belarus, Ukraine, and Poland.

The streets of Riga twist and turn. Local drivers often ignore traffic rules, and this has resulted in Latvia having one of the highest levels of traffic fatalities in Europe.

ENVIRONMENT

A visitor to Kemeri National Park, a protected marshland in Latvia.

CHAPTER 5

L IKE MOST FORMER SOVIET REPUBLICS, Latvia suffers from decades of environmental mismanagement as a result of rapid buildup of heavily polluting industries. In the late 1980s the Latvian government began to talk about protecting the environment as part of the independence movement.

Since regaining independence, Latvia's economy has shifted to service industries, and this has brought benefits to the environment. The

Cargo ships at the port at Riga. The Latvian government is taking steps to manage and minimize pollution from these activities.

The Latvian government is working to preserve and protect the country's flora and fauna. International agreements have been ratified, land protected, and sustainable energy encouraged. Latvia is tackling air and water pollution, caused by decades of neglect and unsafe waste disposal methods practiced by manufacturing and industrial activities.

Gauja National Park. The Latvian government is working to preserve the environment by creating numerous national parks.

government has designated new nature reserves and parks and also has ratified several international agreements on reducing air, water, and land pollution. Wetlands and endangered species are being protected. Sustainable energy consumption tops the list of current environmental priorities. Government subsidies for the insulation of existing buildings are one of the cost-efficient means by which this is being done. Latvia is addressing other important environmental issues, such as improvement of drinking water quality; the sewage system; communal and hazardous water disposal; and reduction of air pollution.

DRINKING WATER AND SEWAGE SYSTEM

The first water supply device was built in Riga in 1620. Water was pumped from an open reservoir and ran through wooden pipes to pools and directly to homes of noblemen. Beginning in 1863, water was drawn from the Daugava River. The quality of water was satisfactory up to the next couple of decades.

Latvians holding balloons that say "Change and Walk" to encourage fellow Latvians to cut down on carbon emissions, and to bring attention to the problem of pollution.

But by the 19th century, the quality of Daugava's water was no longer safe to drink. The river was being polluted by industrial and agricultural waste flowing all the way from Russia and Belarus. After 1904 new water sources had to be found outside Riga. New wells were drilled to meet industrial demands and the needs of an expanding population. The Daugava station in Riga treats and supplies half the drinking water supplied to Riga. The rest comes from groundwater pumped from more than 500 drilled wells. Almost half of Latvia's untreated water contains bacteria of unacceptable safety levels. The environment where groundwater is pumped needs to be improved. Latvia is developing a long-term program to be implemented by 2010 for the more efficient use of groundwater in city water supplies.

During the Soviet era all sewage was discharged into reservoirs adjacent to the district of Riga. Some treatment plants were built in the postwar period.

In the mid-1980s about 7 percent of sewage was treated biologically, and 22 percent mechanically. Since independence in 1991, Latvia implemented a large-scale program to treat its sewage waste. A pressure collector system, large pumping stations, and a biological wastewater treatment plant were installed. At present, about 80 percent of the total sewage amount is biologically treated.

COMMUNAL AND HAZARDOUS WASTE

Under Soviet domination, little attention was paid to the environment in each town. Occupied Latvia invested heavily in the manufacturing industry, but neglected treating hazardous waste. This resulted in the pollution of lakes, rivers, and the Baltic Sea. The Daugava River and the Gulf of Riga reached dangerous levels of pollution from industrial and agricultural chemicals. In 2009 Latvia's first hazardous waste disposal plant began operation in Zebrene, in the Dobele region. It is able to handle 9,000 tons of communal and industrial waste each year.

The waters of the Daugava River were heavily polluted by industrial and agricultural chemicals.

AIR POLLUTION

Emissions of polluting substances in the air promote environmental problems such as acidification, formation of ground-level ozone, and accumulation of hazardous chemical substances in the living organisms. Air pollution is most noticeable in major urban areas where industries are concentrated. Since 1997 the government of Latvia has laid down restrictions on emissions for certain sectors where solvents are used and for emissions of volatile organic compounds from oil depots, fuel filling stations, and especially incineration facilities. Latvia's effort to decrease pollution has effectively reduced the emissions of acidified substances, deposits of sulfur, and nitrogen in 2005.

Smog blankets the city of Riga.

LATVIANS

A Latvian woman in traditional dress.

THE POPULATION OF LATVIA IS about 2.26 million. Latvia's ethnic mix is largely a result of postwar immigration, which led to a decline in the number of ethnic Latvians from 77 percent in 1935 to 52 percent in 1989. The indigenous people of Latvians make up 59.2 percent of 2008 population, while the remainder is made up of a mixture of ethnic groups. Russians make up 28 percent. Minority populations include Belarusians at 3.1 percent, Ukrainians at 2.5 percent, Poles at 2.4 percent, Lithuanians at 1.4 percent, and others at 2 percent.

The Latvian identity is not a unified one, in part due to the differing ethnic groups in the population.

After Latvia regained independence in 1991, citizenship was granted to all pre—World War II citizens and their descendants. Naturalization is relatively easy, requiring five years of residence, a

Right: Latvians are very proud of their heritage.

test of basic-level Latvian language, and a test on the constitution. Numerous surveys have attempted to find why so many people in Latvia (some 16 percent of the total population) choose to remain noncitizens. The majority are Russian-speaking residents. Reasons vary, but about 25 percent of the noncitizens mention ease of travel to Russia as a factor: Visas are expensive for citizens of Latvia, while noncitizens pay only a small fee.

The Latvian Russians are a broad group split into many social classes, with differing economic and political interests. The Russian-speaking citizens tend to vote for two political parties: Harmony and Human Rights, which together win about 25 percent of the vote in parliamentary elections. Most of the elected council members are local businesspeople. Many Russians work in the industrial sector, with a few in agriculture. Some of the younger generation of Russians are very active in business and enterprise.

Despite Latvia's separation from Russia, many Russians have chosen to stay in what has become their homeland.

ETHNIC MINORITIES

RUSSIANS Russians were the largest minority in Latvia after World War I, making up about 10 percent of the population in 1935. Refugees from Russia after the Bolshevik Revolution created a vibrant community in Riga, with a daily newspaper, theater, and many other cultural activities.

By 1935 there were 206,499 Russians in Latvia. Several hundred thousand ethnic Russians entered Latvia immediately after World War II, and a steady stream of immigration continued into the 1980s. By 1989 the number had increased to 905,515. In the years after Latvia regained independence, a wave of Russian immigration began to take place; between 1992 and 1994 some 62,000 returned to Russia. By 2006 almost half of the population in Riga was made up of Russians (42.3 percent), and in the second-largest city, Daugavpils, over half the population (53.3 percent) was Russian.

Latvian Russians are culturally united by their use of the Russian language, rather than by their nationality. Russian intellectuals have

Women lighting candles in the Russian Orthodox church in Riga.

formed a number of organizations to promote Russian culture and education in Latvia. The two main Russian-speaking political parties represented in the national parliament and municipal governments are the Harmony Center, which is a coalition of four center-left parties, and For Human Rights, a left-wing political party.

The Latvian Russian Cultural Center, founded in 1994, united seven Russian organizations, including the Russian Children's Choir and the Russian Folk Instruments Orchestra. Some Russian organizations are also working in the opposite direction by introducing Latvian culture to the Russian population.

In a number of schools in Latvia the curriculum is taught in Russian, but this has begun to change since independence in Latvia. These schools are giving up the standardized Russian curriculum forced on them during the Soviet period and are concentrating on establishing an independent Russian language stream within the Latvian national educational system.

The Poles are mostly city dwellers concentrated in Riga and Daugavpils.

UKRAINIANS As of 2004 Ukrainians made up 2.6 percent of the population of Latvia. Most of them live in the city of Liepāja and have not really integrated into Latvian society. Under 17 percent of them speak Latvian, and most consider Russian their native tongue, rather than Ukrainian.

Many Ukrainians in Latvia are former officers from the Soviet army. Most of them have undergone retraining and are employed in other areas now, although more than 25,000 Ukrainians left Latvia after the disintegration of the Soviet Union.

POLES Poles have been long-time residents of Latvia and are considered one of Latvia's traditional minorities. The number of Poles in the country has barely changed in the last 100 years, including the last 50 years under Soviet occupation.

Two-thirds of the people of Polish origin are now Latvian citizens, and most are fluent in Latvian. The Poles have strong cultural traditions and a great interest in maintaining the traditions of Polish culture. Every year hundreds of pupils participate in concerts organized by Polish societies and also the cultural events in Poland.

LITHUANIANS As of 2007 Lithuanians made up 1.4 percent of Latvia's population, of which the largest concentration is found in the towns of

History is a vital part of the education of Latvia's young generations. Children of various ethnicities attend school together.

Saldus, Bauska, and Liepāja. A high percentage of Lithuanians are engaged in farming, and most have integrated into Latvia. More than half of Lithuanians speak Latvian, and there is a high rate of intermarriage.

GERMANS Germans in Latvia occupy a special place among the ethnic minority groups, given that settlers of German descent have lived in the Baltic territories since the 13th century. Over the centuries up to independence in 1918, they have continued to hold the upper levels of authority in the country.

The Germanic influence on Latvian culture remained very strong until Latvia gained its independence in 1918. At that time many Germans left Latvia, unable to reconcile themselves to the loss of their former privileges and social status. According to the Russian Empire census of 1897, Germans in Latvia accounted for 6.2 percent of Latvia's population. By 1935, the German population had dropped to half of what it had been at the turn of the century. Since 1959, the number of resident Germans has increased, mainly due to Germans moving to Latvia from Russia. Presently 0.2 percent of Latvia's population is German.

JEWS There are about 11,000 Jews in Riga. Smaller communities are in Daugavpils (Dvinsk). The community is small but active. Synagogues are found in Riga, Daugavpils, Liepāja, and Rezhitsa. About 500 children learn both Hebrew and Yiddish in a Jewish school in Riga. A prominent Latvian of Jewish heritage today is Gidon Kremer, internationally acclaimed violinist.

The first Jewish colony in Latvia was established in Piltene in 1571. The Jews contributed to Latvia's development until the Northern War (1700—1721), which greatly reduced Latvia's population. In the 18th century Jews from Prussia reestablished themselves in Latvia and played a significant role in its economy. In independent Latvia, the Jewish community flourished. Jews formed political parties and some became members of parliament.

Before World War II, there were about 85,000 Jews in Latvia. By the end of the war, more than 90 percent of Latvian Jews had perished. Latvian Jews today are the descendants of survivors of Jews who fled to the Soviet Union to escape the Nazi invasion and later returned, or came to Latvia from other parts of the Soviet Union after the war. Those who are not descendants of prewar residents are unable to enjoy full civil rights.

THE CHANGING SOCIAL STRUCTURE

Until the 19th century the main occupation in Latvia was agriculture. Most Latvians lived in the countryside as peasants, and there were no class distinctions, because everyone lived off the land from the labor of their own hands. Those who lived in the towns and cities were small tradesmen, craftsmen, and artisans. The landowners or barons, who were mostly German, held all the power in local municipalities, and even the local clergymen were controlled by them.

With the coming of the first National Awakening in the second part of the 19th century, some Latvians became teachers and ministers and moved into positions of power and responsibility. Some rural Latvians moved to the cities and became involved in trade as owners of businesses and of property. With the development of factories at the end of the 19th century, an industrial working class of Latvians also developed in the cities.

During the period of Soviet occupation, society was dominated by the Communist Party. After Eduards Berklāvs and other "national Communists" were removed from government in 1959, leadership shifted to the Russian governing class, while the Latvian population moved back to a lower level in the social structure.

Today on Latvia's streets there is evidence of the progress that Latvian nationals have made into the higher echelons of society.

SOCIAL CLASSES

During the years of independence from 1918 to 1941, the typical social classes of a democratic society evolved—farmers, farm laborers, and small tradesmen in the countryside, and entrepreneurs and workers, along with artists, writers, actors, intellectuals, and bureaucrats in the cities. After regaining independence, Latvians are slowly moving into all levels of society again, although the Russians from the former communist regime continued to dominate the economy.

The entrepreneurial class is the most powerful. Several leading entrepreneurs are active in politics, as leaders of political parties, or elected officials. However, the turnover of political elites has been very high. Farmers are in the most difficult situation. The breakup of the collective farms and movement back to small family farms has presented many difficulties—a lack of farming skills and farming equipment, soil that has been depleted over decades, a lack of farm buildings, and the total lack of infrastructure. To top it off, farmers have to compete in agricultural production with the warmer climates of southern European Union member states and overcome protectionist policies in potential markets.

Bales of hay on a farm. Farmers have found it difficult to keep afloat in the face of a lack of modern farming equipment and techniques and an increase in competition.

TRADITIONAL FINERY

Historically, one of the most conspicuous examples of Latvian national identity was the production of fabrics and garments. Fabric was woven in every peasant homestead. During the feudal era, Latvians were forced to wear national dress and forbidden to wear fashionable clothes. The national dress was supposed to be evidence of the wearer's membership in the lower class. Nevertheless, the bright and varied colors of traditional garments livened up the bleak dreariness of their daily lives.

The classic traditional Latvian folk dress dates back to the 7th to 13th century, and making it is a living art that is practiced to this day. The design, choice of fabrics, and ornamentation used has remained unchanged over the centuries, and the style of the dress has been preserved from generation to generation.

The basic design of the national dress is the same from region to region, but the color and ornamentation varies.

FAMOUS LATVIAN PEOPLE

KRIŠJĀNIS VALDEMĀRS (1825–91) Krišjānis Valdemārs was the leader of the first National Awakening movement. He was one of those responsible for publishing the first newspaper in Latvian from Saint Petersburg. Valdemārs encouraged Latvians to take pride in their language and history. He urged the peasants to buy land and thus gain financial independence. Moreover, he established a maritime school and advised coastal inhabitants to engage themselves in shipping.

ULJANA SEMJONOVA (1952) Uljana Semjonova was born in Medumi, a village in the Daugavpils district. At 7 feet (2.13 m) tall Semjonova was the leading women's basketball player in the world in the 1970s and 1980s. She won the championships 15 times each for both the Soviet Union and the European Champion's Cup. Semjonova is a three-time world champion in female basketball, and she has won two Olympic gold medals while playing for the Soviet Union in 1976 and 1980. She never lost a game in an official international competition.

VAIRA VĪĶE-FREIBERGA (1937–) Vaira VīĶe was born in Riga. During the Soviet occupation, her family fled the country and became refugees in Germany and later French Morocco. In 1954 young Vaira arrived in Canada. There she earned a bachelor's degree in 1958 and a master's degree in 1960, both in psychology. The same year, Vaira married Professor Imants Freibergs. In 1965 she earned a doctorate in experimental psychology.

Vīĸe-Freiberga is proficient in Latvian, English, French, German, and Spanish, and was active in community service, focusing on questions of Latvian identity and culture, and the political future of the Baltic States. In 1998 she was elected professor emeritus at the University of Montreal and

President Vaira Vīĸe-Freiberga (*right*) with her Swiss counterpart, Micheline Calmy-Rey (*left*).

LATVIA'S FIRST PRIME MINISTER

Kārlis Ulmanis (1877—1942) was Latvia's first prime minister and the last before the Soviet occupation in 1940. The youngest of three brothers, he was born and raised on a farm and took up agricultural studies in Switzerland and East Prussia, becoming very active in advocating modern farming techniques in Latvia. From 1907 to 1909 he attended school in the United States, graduating from the University of Nebraska.

Returning to Latvia, Ulmanis founded the Latvian Farmers Union, and became the party's leader. It was one of several political groupings to voice the idea of an independent Latvia. It finally got the chance to put theory into action in 1918 when representatives of various organizations and parties formed the National Council after World War I. The council proclaimed a sovereign Latvian state and appointed Kārlis Ulmanis as the prime minister.

In 1934 Ulmanis suspended the constitution and dismissed the Saeima, suspending all political parties. The political party with the largest voter support, the Latvian Social Democratic Workers Party, opposed the coup. He arrested its leaders and other potential political opponents. Ulmanis quickly established political censorship of the mass media and concentrated all power in the hands of the cabinet, headed by himself. The economic policy that Ulmanis then put in place had much in common with that of the New Deal in the United States, resulting in considerable progress in agriculture, successful development of industry, stable government spending, and a relatively high standard of living for the population.

With the occupation of Latvia by the Soviet Union, Ulmanis was deported to Siberia where he died in a prison camp in 1942. His name will be closely tied forever with Latvia's first real period of independence, as he was one of the major forces in achieving democracy, as well as overturning it.

returned to Latvia. In October of that year, she was appointed the director of the newly founded Latvian Institute. On June 17, 1999, she was elected president of the Republic of Latvia by the parliament (Saeima). In 2003 she was re-elected for a second term of four years, winning 88 votes out of 96. Vīķe-Freiberga has received many medals and other honors for distinguished work in the humanities and social sciences. Three biographies about Vīķe-Freiberga have been published in Latvian, English, French, Spanish, Italian, Finnish, and Russian.

LIFESTYLE

Pedestrians on the crosswalk just outside the National Theater.

CHAPTER 7

THE SOUL OF THE LATVIAN IS TIED to the care of the land and the soil. A Latvian proverb illustrates this feeling perfectly: "He who cares for the land will be fed by the land." This attachment to the soil is evident in much of Latvian tradition, as well as in their literature, painting, music, and sculpture.

The makeup of the extended Latvian family is similar to that in other Western countries—father, mother, children, grandparents, aunts, and

Young mothers with their children.

Latvians have close links to the land as evidenced by how many urban Latvians tend gardens. Latvians often have close ties with their families. Women are considered the glue that holds the family together and the ones who pass down traditions. Now many young Latvians are moving to the cities in search for better employment and access to modern conveniences.

uncles—and family ties are usually strong. Two children is considered the ideal, and they are usually born and brought up in the family home where they are taught to assume the roles that they will play later in life.

Since Latvia regained its independence, women have the same legal rights as men. However, much remains to be done for true equality to emerge, as women are not proportionally represented in politics—very few women are nominated and even fewer are elected.

LATVIAN WOMEN

Women make up of the majority of the population of Latvia. According to a 2009 population estimate, there were 797,505 women compared with 756,469 men between the ages of 15 and 74. Women also made up 62.9 percent of the workforce. Almost one-third of all working women are employed in the education and health services.

Women are entitled to 16 weeks of paid maternity leave. They can extend that for another 18 months of unpaid parental leave and still hold onto

Women in Latvia shoulder the main responsibility for the management of the household and for the care and upbringing of the children.

their jobs. Life expectancy for women is longer than for men. In 2009 life expectancy was 77.5 years for females and 67 years for males.

In more traditional Latvian society, men continue to play a dominant role. The majority of public officials and leaders are men, although more and more women are assuming managerial positions. Men also continue to be regarded as the head of the family.

Several people affected Latvian perceptions of women dramatically. Prominent among them is Vaira Vīķe-Freiberga who was elected president (1999—2007). Sandra Kalniete, whose credentials include art historian and author, was Latvia's EU commissioner (2004), ambassador to the UN (1993—97), party leader of Civic Union, and elected member of the European Parliament (2009). Marie N (Marija Naumova) is a popular singer who won the Eurovision Song Competition in 2002. She is popular among ethnic Latvians and ethnic Russians alike; her ethnic heritage is Russian.

Sandra Kalniete is one woman who has altered the Latvian perspective of women.

THE OLDER GENERATIONS Older people still have an important role in passing on traditions to the next generation, because they are usually the guardians of customs and beliefs and the holders of knowledge and wisdom. Unfortunately, many elderly people live below the poverty line. During the transition period after regaining independence, the Latvian government was unable to improve this situation by increasing pensions. The average old-age pension in 1995 was only about 35 percent of the average wage. As a result elderly people often become dependent on their children to maintain their standard of living. Approximately 17 percent of the population of Latvia is 65 years or over (2008 estimate).

URBAN AND RURAL LIVING

Rural living dwindled from 34 percent of the total population in 2005 to 32 percent in 2008. Young people flock to the cities for better-paying

Many elderly people in Latvia live below the poverty line.

jobs, an improved living environment, and access to various services. The majority of Latvians in urban areas live in below-standard housing, due to the construction and ownership of all accommodations by the state during Soviet rule. The apartments built during this period were of very poor quality and received limited maintenance over the 50-year period. Apartments had only one or two rooms, a small kitchen, and a bathroom that was often shared with other families. Houses built before the Soviet occupation may have been of better quality, but many have not been maintained properly and have deteriorated beyond repair.

With the regaining of independence and the reinstatement of private ownership of property, there is extensive renovation being carried out on older private homes, apartments, farms, and public buildings, as well as the construction of new ones. Some people own their apartments, which they have been able to buy in new, privately owned buildings.

During the Soviet period, each citizen was officially allocated six square yards (five square meters) of living space. The majority of city dwellers still live in relatively small apartments.

SELF-SUFFICIENCY

During the Soviet period, the urban garden was often a necessity to supplement the meager food supplies with basics such as potatoes, onions, and cabbage, and it continues to play the same role to some extent. However, spiritually, the garden is to the city dweller what the cottage is to the North American—a place to relax, to sit in the sun, and to get out of close living quarters in the city.

In the countryside, the collective farm system that existed during the Soviet era is gradually disappearing, although most country people continue to live in Soviet-era central housing complexes, which are located well away from the fields. Many families are now returning to rejuvenated single-family farms, reconstructing the farm buildings and learning subsistence farming methods, as a high percentage of these small farms still lack electricity, farm machinery, and proper facilities for the farm animals.

Agriculture was traditionally the mainstay of the Latvian economy, and some people say that agriculture should still be the main thrust of the government's economic policy today. This belief, however, is not shared by those living in urban areas.

During Soviet rule, many Latvians had small gardens to supplement their meager food supplies.

NEW BIRTH

Latvia's mortality rate for newborn babies is close to 10 per 1,000 births (2009). For a Latvian family, the arrival of a newborn child is a time for much celebration. Parents usually appoint relatives as godparents, in the belief that children inherit their godparents' good qualities. A baby girl may have two godmothers and one godfather, and a baby boy may have two godfathers and one godmother. Traditionally the baby's name is announced

Latvian parents at the name-giving ceremony for their new baby.

during a formal ceremony (called *Krustaba*) in which the godparents promise to care for the child in the event that the parents cannot. The newly named child is then introduced to the guests and welcomed as a full-fledged member of the family.

MARRIAGE

Another major event is the wedding, which usually begins with a formal proposal of marriage. A century or more ago, this was done through intermediaries speaking to the mother of the bride-to-be and then to her father and brothers. Once the proposal was accepted, a party was held at the bride's house, which often lasted right through the night. Nowadays it is up to the bride and the groom to decide how their wedding should be celebrated.

Today the modern wedding ceremony often takes place in a church, where the bride gets married wearing traditional white and attended by bridesmaids. The bride and groom often invite another couple (*vedēji*), usually older than them, to lead them into church, and lead the celebrations afterward. Wedding celebrations often last for three days—even lasting for over a week in some cases!

The singing of special songs is an important part of the wedding ritual. After the church ceremonies, a feast is held during which the newlyweds are initiated as married people. The bride's coronet is replaced with a headdress commonly worn by married women, and the bridegroom is offered a hat appropriate for married men. A shawl is then placed over the shoulders of the couple, and the guests sing them a song of welcome to married life.

A TRADITIONAL LATVIAN WEDDING

The festivities of a traditional Latvian wedding begin when representatives of the bridegroom go to the house of the bride to bring her to the groom's house for the ceremony. The bride—dressed in her finest clothes—says good-bye to all the people she has lived with at her parents' house, giving them small gifts. Then she leaves with her escort to travel to the groom's

A newly married couple shares a kiss on a bridge in Kronvalda Park, where couples attach locks of hair to ensure a long and happy marriage.

A freshly baked loaf of bread is offered to the bridal couple to symbolize unity.

house. Once she is there, a formal ceremony is held in which vows and rings are exchanged, and the bride's coronet, which symbolizes her maidenhood, is replaced by a headscarf, worn by all married women. After this a special meal is prepared for everyone to enjoy. In times of economic difficulty, the fall months were a popular time to get married, when food was plentiful.

HEALTH

The recent long years spent under Soviet dominance have resulted in poor living conditions in Latvia and the neglect of health. The birthrate is low (9.78 births per 1,000 population), and the death rate—especially infant mortality—is high (8.77 deaths per 1,000 population). Overall life expectancy is 72 years, compared to 81 years in neighboring Sweden.

In general the lifestyle of the Latvian population also contributes to poor health, with high levels of alcohol consumption, smoking, and unhealthy diets.

In one Latvian wedding custom, groomsmen "kidnap" the bride, and the groom must complete a simple task, such as singing a song or consuming a round of drinks, to "ransom" her back. In another Latvian tradition, a couple writes their sins on small rocks before tossing them into a body of water to atone for their sins. This ritual is sometimes performed before weddings.

Latvia has a state-supported health plan for all inhabitants, but a large proportion of medical costs are currently paid by patients themselves, as the health system, similar to all other social systems, is currently in a period of transition, and government financial resources are still inadequate. This often means that cancer and other illnesses are diagnosed late, increasing the cost of treatment and reducing the chances of recovery. Diseases that can be linked to poor social conditions, such as sexually transmitted diseases, continue to increase.

Health education is limited, and so those responsible for paying their own medical costs choose other necessities for the family over their own well-being.

Latvia's current public health strategy is based on the WHO Health for All Framework that was adopted in 2001 by the cabinet of ministers.

EDUCATION

Latvians begin their education at seven years of age. The compulsory (basic) education lasts nine years, although preschool attendance is voluntary, as not all schools provide kindergartens. About 99.5 percent of Latvian people age 15 and over are able to read and write.

The first law establishing compulsory education for all children was passed in 1919. The language of instruction was the language spoken in the family. The compulsory foreign language was at first German, although it was later replaced by English. The state also finances ethnic minority schools or classes where courses are taught in Belorusian, Estonian, Hebrew, Lithuanian, Polish, Roma, Russian, and Ukrainian.

Latvia places a high priority on education. Education up to secondary school is free, and scholarships are offered for higher education. About two-thirds of secondary school graduates continue with higher education. Latvia had 60 colleges and institutions of higher education in 2007, most of which belonged to the state; the rest were founded by legal entities or private individuals.

Kindergarten children doing their morning exercise routine.

A BROADER CURRICULUM

After World War II, during the period of Soviet occupation, the Latvian school system was sovietized, and the curriculum was changed according to socialist political theories. The teaching of Latvian language and history diminished, and the number of Russian schools increased. Riga Medical Institute was established in 1950, and the Civil Aviation Engineering Institute was also founded in 1960. Now that Latvia has regained its independence, the general structure of these educational institutions has been maintained. Latvian history and literature are taught without "political revisions," and Latvian has become the main language of instruction.

The teaching process was also changed with the regaining of independence, moving away from central control of all subjects that were taught to more autonomy within each school. Within guidelines established by the state, schools may vary their curriculum and choose their own teaching methods. The students are taught and encouraged to seek greater personal initiative, independence, and responsibility.

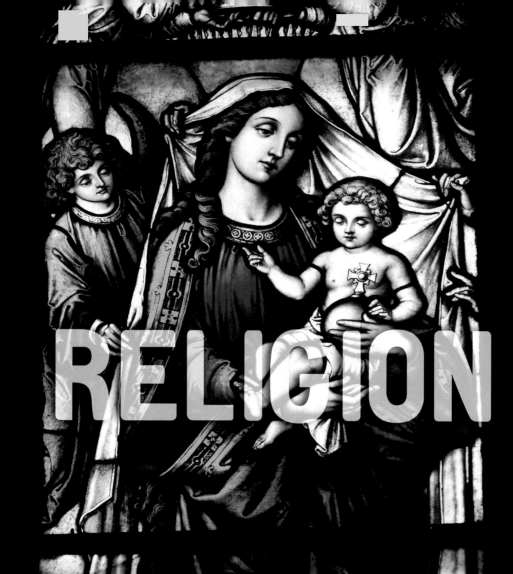

RELIGION

A stained glass window in the
Lutheran Cathedral.

M

ANY OF LATVIA'S RELIGIOUS
beliefs and traditions began in
ancient times and were passed
down through the generations, partly
to appease supernatural forces and
increase the fertility of the land, and in
part to improve personal welfare and
commemorate joyous and tragic events.

Worshipers of Latvia's ancient religions gathered at traditional places
such as "holy" hills and lakes as well as groves of oak or lime trees. All

Schoolchildren and their teacher sing an ancient religious folk song.

Before the
introduction of
Christianity by
German monks
and crusaders
in the early
1200s, Latvians
worhiped three
divine beings
out of a pantheon
of 5,000 gods.
Over time, these
ancient beliefs
were assimilated
into Christianity.
When Latvia
became
independent,
the church and
state were
separated and
religious freedom
was reinstated.

of creation was viewed as a harmonious entity, to be respected and honored. There were some 5,000 original gods, but only three were worshiped as divine beings—Dievs, Māra, and Laima. Worship of these deities goes back a long way. Over time these old beliefs have been mixed with Christian beliefs, and the original traditions are not always obvious, but there is extensive use of the symbols as design elements in textiles, metals, pottery, and wood. Latvians no longer practice the ancient religion, but the tradition lives on in folk songs, legends, and festivals.

CHRISTIANITY

Christianity was introduced to Latvia in the early 1200s by Eastern Orthodox and Roman Catholic monks and crusaders of the Teutonic Order. Originally, services were held in Latin, and so they were not understood by the Latvians, causing the new religion to spread slowly. It was accepted on the surface, but the familiar traditions and ways held for centuries were continued in secret. Latvians' adherence to their own religious ways was tied closely to the need for continuing resistance against the conquering foreigners.

Church towers dominate the skyline of Old Town in Riga.

LATVIAN CHURCHES

Among the best-known and finest examples of Latvian church architecture is the Riga Dome Cathedral, known as Rigas Doms. Started in 1211 by the Germanic Bishop Albert I, the original building was in the Romanesque style with round arches, many of which survive to this day. It was added to in the Gothic style during the next two centuries—the pointed arches built next to the round ones and new structures, such as side chapels and a west transept, were constructed. In the 18th century more additions were made in the Baroque style, and in the 20th century a new entrance hall was built. The cathedral also contains magnificent stained glass windows depicting themes from the Bible and the history of Riga.

CATHOLICISM

The spread of Christianity was tied to the strengthening of German rule in Livonia and the creation of the dominating ruling classes.

Colorful murals on the interior of a Russian Orthodox church.

The Catholic faith was introduced into Latvia in 1186 when Meinhard, a German monk, became the first bishop. He built a wooden church to begin his missionary work, but he met with almost no success at first. His successor, Berthold of Hanover, was appointed bishop of Livonia, but he was killed in battle soon after he arrived in 1198.

It was not until the arrival of Bishop Albert of Buxhoeveden, who succeeded Berthold as bishop, nearly 20 years after Meinhard arrived, that the real conversion of the Latvians to Christianity began. This may have been in part due to his entourage of 23 ships of armed crusaders. Alberts also secured an alliance with King Valdemar of Denmark, who landed in Tallinn with an army in 1219.

The Jesuits attempted to continue the spread of Catholicism after the bishopric ceased to exist in 1563, but with the spread of the Reformation into Latvia soon after, the Catholic Church quickly lost its influence over most of Latvia, except in the eastern Latgale region.

THE PROTESTANT REFORMATION

The Protestant Reformation started in Riga in 1521 and soon spread throughout Livonia. Lutheranism—the movement adhering to the doctrine of Martin Luther, the leader of the Protestant Reformation in Germany—in particular was further consolidated under 17th-century Swedish domination. The clergy wielded comprehensive influence and power over all aspects of daily life, particularly during the feudal period. Permission was necessary for all important acts of one's life, such as the choice of a husband or wife, the date for the marriage, the choice of names for children at baptism, or even permission to attend school.

RELIGIOUS FREEDOM

By the time the Republic of Latvia was established in 1918, there were three principal religious denominations in the country—Lutheran, Roman Catholic, and Russian Orthodox.

Ernst Gluck, a Lutheran clergyman who was the first translator of the Bible into Latvian, also founded the first Latvian-language school in Vidzeme in 1683. The Russian army captured the town during the Great Northern War (1702) and deported its entire population, including Gluck and his foster daughter, Marta Skavronska. She later became Empress Catherine I of Russia.

The church was separated from the state, and offenses against an individual's beliefs were forbidden by law. During the years of Soviet occupation, religious freedom for all faiths was suppressed. There was large-scale deportation of clergy, and church property was seized by the state. Some churches were turned into concert halls, museums, warehouses, movie theaters, and meeting halls, while others were burned or left to ruin. Membership in all congregations fell dramatically, although the Catholic Church lost fewer members than the Lutherans.

With the regaining of independence in 1991, religious life returned and is flourishing. Religious freedom has been reinstated, and the rights of religious organizations are guaranteed by law. Congregations have regained the use of their former properties, and churches are being restored.

A 13th-century Lutheran church.

LANGUAGE

A magazine and newspaper stand in Riga.

CHAPTER 9

LATVIAN HAS CONSTITUTIONAL status as the official language of Latvia and is used in all spheres of activity, although any other language may be used in government meetings by agreement.

Latvian is also the dominant language of the mass media, although newspapers, broadcasts, and films are also produced in Russian, English, and Swedish. Most people have cable television, which brings in programs from many countries and languages.

Children in a Latvian-language class.

Latvian is the official language of Latvia and is extensively used in all aspects of life. While under German and Russian rule, the use of Latvian was discouraged and has only developed as a modern language in the early 20th century. Latvian has been heavily influenced by German due to Germany's occupation in earlier times. It has also been influenced by Finnish, French, and Polish.

The Latvian language comes from an ancient Indo-European language family that was spoken at about the same time as ancient Greek, Latin, and Sanskrit. Over the centuries it has been influenced by other languages with which the ancient Latvians came into contact, especially Livonian (now nearly extinct) and Old Russian, which added words related to the church and the law courts.

Two men, Juris Alunāns (1832—64) and Atis Kronvalds (1837—75), made the greatest contributions to the development of a standard Latvian language and uniting literary language and the spoken idioms of the Latvian dialects. Standard Latvian is the official language of Latvia.

HISTORICAL DEVELOPMENT

In contrast to the language of neighboring Lithuania, Latvian has undergone extensive changes over the last few centuries. The largest addition to the Latvian vocabulary came during the Middle Ages from Middle Low German, which added words in the fields of crafts, fashion, and agriculture. Some very archaic words—for example, *asins* (an original Indo-European word for "blood")—have been preserved. Through trade, wars, and invasions, Latvian has been exposed to the influence of many other languages and cultures, including Finnish, Polish, French, English, and Russian.

Until the 19th century the development of Latvian language and literature was mainly in the hands of German clergymen. Many of them learned

A Russian conversing with a Latvian. Each nationality speaks at least a little of the other's language.

and understood the Latvian peasant language and attempted to keep the influence of their native German on Latvian writing to a reasonable level. As a result, no real separation ever developed between the literary language and popular speech.

The most significant period of development for modern Latvian as it is spoken and written today started early in the 20th century. For the first time, Latvian became the principal language of Latvia, although during the long period of occupation, both Latvian and Russian were considered official languages and the use of Latvian was discouraged.

LANGUAGE IN LITERATURE

The 19th century was an important period for the development of both the Latvian written and spoken language. It saw the rise of Latvian national literature, which was the first conscious effort of the Latvians themselves to care for their language. Words were coined for the new notions of Western civilization, a necessary process when a peasant idiom was developing into a cultural language.

The development of Latvian was further strengthened through new literary works—especially those of Jānis Rainis, who used his numerous translations of Western European classics to help create new means of expression for his poetry, using words that eventually became part of the language.

Rainis's works were famous for their assertion of national freedom and social consciousness. He was arrested and sent to eastern Russia from Latvia in 1897 because of his socialist political activities, but returned in 1903 to take part in the unsuccessful revolution of 1905. He then left for Switzerland and did not return again until 1920 after Latvia's first independence had been secured. On his return he was elected to the Saeima as the minister of education and director of the National Theater.

Rainis translated many international literary works, including Goethe's *Faust* and works by Schiller, Shakespeare, Heine, and Pushkin. These translations extended the Latvian vocabulary and also introduced the usage

The National Theater in Riga.

of shorter word forms. His original works were inspired by historical and international themes. A masterpiece, "Joseph and His Brothers," is based on a theme of prophecy and forgiveness that appears in the Christian Old Testament and Jewish Talmud.

MODERNIZING LATVIAN

After the country gained independence in 1918, new needs arose for its development into a republic with its own identity. Latvian terminology needed to be developed for the law courts, the administrative system, and for the newly established university, art academy, and music conservatory. Official Latvian place names were also needed to replace the old czarist Russian ones.

Present-day standard written Latvian uses a 33-letter alphabet, based on Latin origins. Modern Latvian is expressive and versatile, and is suited for poetry and literature as well as for sophisticated scientific texts.

A well-stocked library in Riga.

Presently approximately 62 percent of Latvia's people are native speakers of Latvian, and it is spoken by approximately 1.4 million people, although Russian continues to be commonly heard on the streets of Riga. Latvian is spoken as a first language by minority populations in Russia, the United States, Canada, Ireland, Australia, South America, and other European Union countries.

THE ROLE OF THE MEDIA

The media play an important role in affecting the tone and usage of the two main languages in Latvia—Latvian and Russian. Currently approximately 100 periodicals are published in Latvia, of which some 60 newspapers and magazines are published in Riga. Newspaper circulation figures are fairly small, and the readerships are concentrated around the main cities.

There are five national newspapers. *Diena*, a national daily published six days a week in Latvian, has a circulation of about 55,000. Comparatively Russian newspapers have a much lower circulation. The popular newspaper *Vesti seqodnia* (*Today's News*) has a circulation of about 35,000. A free

Latvians buying newspapers from a vendor.

newspaper called *5 min*, published by the Diena Group, aims to reach people who rarely or never read newspapers and targets the Russian-speaking majority in Riga especially. It has a daily circulation of 100,000. There are about 190 monthly and weekly women's magazines offered for subscription.

LATVIAN GRAMMAR

The earliest texts in Latvian appeared in the 16th century, and the first grammar was developed two centuries later. Jānis Endzelins, the most noted Latvian philologist, laid the foundation of modern Latvian grammar and vocabulary through his research and the publication of the book *Latvian Grammar*, which created new words and clarified others.

Present-day written Latvian uses a macron, a mark placed over vowels to indicate vowel length, and an accent over or under a consonant to indicate the softer pronunciation of a letter. There are three Latvian dialect groups—East (or High), West, and Central.

RADIO AND TELEVISION

Some 36 national, Riga, local, or regional radio stations and two state-funded TV stations broadcast regularly in Latvian and/or Russian. Latvian Radio broadcasts in Latvian and Russian, with newscasts in German and English, as well as in the languages of Latvia's ethnic minorities. A total of 85 percent of the population listens to radio at least once a week. Russian state radio is received in Latvia, as are programs from the *Voice of America* and *Radio Free Europe*.

Latvian state television was established in 1954. An independent channel was established in 1992, with nightly news broadcasts in Latvian and English. Russian state television and a private channel from Moscow also broadcast in Latvia. Cable and satellite television brings in many international broadcasts. The nightly news program, *Panorama*, is the most popular program and is essential viewing for many Latvians.

A TV tower in Riga.

ARTS

A sculpture at Folklore Park.

C ULTURE IN LATVIA IS ANCIENT AND dates back to the years before the country was invaded and swamped by the heritage of other nations. Latvia lost its cultural identity during the long years of foreign dominance, but since independence the vitality of its arts has reappeared in many different forms.

The arts thrive through drama groups, choirs, ensembles, orchestras, and dance groups. Latvians are immensely proud of their heritage and,

Women and children performing a dance.

A statue of Jānis Rainis.

especially since independence in 1991, strive to express themselves and their identity through prose, plays, and music.

Latvia is famous for its song festivals, which have been in existence since the 1870s. They are popular events in Latvia, as well as in Latvian immigrant communities throughout the world. Several thousand singers take part in the festivals.

Every few years, local towns and districts hold competitions for choirs, orchestras, and dance groups to select the best for a national festival.

LITERATURE

Although Latvian culture is ancient, its literature is relatively new, having only come into its own during the National Awakening of 1850 to 1880. Before this time nearly all writing about Latvia was done by foreigners, mainly Baltic Germans.

In 1878 the first classic novel in Latvian, *Mērnieku laiki*, was published. It was a comic satire of country life filled with caricatures of stereotypical Latvians such as the devout hypocrite, the old gossiper, and others written by two brothers, Reinis and Matiss Kaudzitis, who spent 20 years writing it. In 1888 the national epic "*Lāčplēsis*" (*Bearslayer*), written by Andrejs Pumpurs, based on Latvian folklore was published. In 1890 a new era in Latvian literature called the *Jaunā strāva* (*New Current*) began in which contemporary problems through the imagery of folk poetry were depcited. The most prominent writer of this period was Jānis Plieksans (1865—1929) who used the pen name Jānis Rainis. He was born into a well-to-do family. However, he edited a socialist newspaper, and for his activities in the political underground he was arrested, imprisoned and then banished from Latvia for 20 years. Rainis's wife, Aspazija (1868—1943), was a well-known author in the 1890s of numerous blockbuster plays with radical feminist themes. In her days, she was recognized as the leading writer of modern Latvian literature. Between them they laid the foundation for modern Latvian drama, journalism, and literature. Rudolfs Blaumanis (1863—1908) is perhaps Latvia's greatest playwright. He influenced young Latvian writers and authors to raise standards in the language and writing style of the Latvian language. Although he is best known for his tragedies, he wrote comedies as well. His characters are set in an everyday environment, and their powerful conflicts related to alcoholism, love and money, and general change formed the plot of his plays.

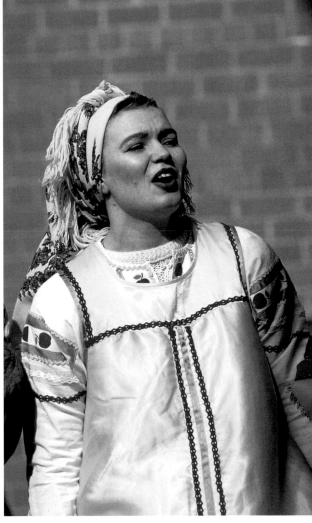

Kārlis Skalbe (1879—1945), who was known as the Latvian Hans Christian Andersen, wrote rich nationalistic verses and fairy tales. He was the youngest of ten children and grew up in poverty. He too lived in exile for his anti-czarist activities and was one of the first intellectuals to openly discuss the idea of full independence for Latvia.

After Latvia gained independence in 1918, a new period in Latvian literature and drama began, as the literary climate was stimulating, intellectual, and creative. Realism continued to be popular in literature, as were themes that glorified the past, although love themes also become quite popular. Short stories gained popularity in the early 1920s. New newspapers and magazines appeared.

A Latvian actress during a performance. Latvians are proud to be able to display their literary and artistic talents freely.

A stage performer taking part in a summer festival.

The best-known author of this period—and also considered Latvia's greatest modern poet—is Aleksandrs Čaks. He disregarded rhyme and used daring and unexpected images. Although his choice of topics was considered shocking at the time, his poems of the 1930s stand out as remarkable works of art.

This period ended with the occupation of Latvia by the Soviets in the 1940s. Under the Soviet occupation, the sole aim of Latvian literature was to praise communism and Stalinism, so literary work became dull and mainly took the form of industrial and agricultural narratives. Nevertheless, after censorship was relaxed somewhat in the late 1950s, a number of well-known Latvian writers were able to practice their craft throughout the years of Soviet occupation, even though some of them suffered greatly from persecution. Some of the better known include the novelist Alberts Bels, and poet Vizma Belsevica. In the 1980s and 1990s, literature in Latvia was no longer subjected to political censorship. Readers had free access to works written in exile by authors such as Astrī de Ivaska, Roberts Muks, Andrejs Eglitis, and Margita Gutmane. The works of authors and poets such as Knuts Skujenieks (*Seed in the Snow*) and Bronislava Martuževa (*Roadside Crosses*) who had been deported or imprisoned during the Soviet era were published.

Literature in the 21st century has branched out into various genres for readers of the independence years. Realistic narratives, fiction, and documentary literature that depict memories of deportation or tragic fates of families in the occupation years are gaining popularity. Sandra Kalniete's

With Dancing Shoes in Siberian Snows has been translated into nine languages. The trilogy *Bille* by Vizma Belsevica recounts memories of childhood in 1930s and 1940s.

LITERARY WORK ON THE STAGE

After Stalin's death in 1953, there was a small revival of pre-Soviet Latvian culture, such as folk songs and folktales, and some literary works of past writers were legalized again. Some of the Latvian writers who had been deported to Siberia were also allowed to return to Latvia and write again.

At the end of the Soviet occupation, the poet Māra Zālīte turned the classic Latvian epic, *Lacplesis*, into a rock opera in which the national hero exemplified nonviolent political action, and the prose of Regina Ezers began to deal with the topic of sensitive individuals isolated and destroyed by a totalitarian environment. Vizma Belsevica, a contemporary novelist, was even considered for the Nobel Prize for Literature in 1992.

Latvian actors during a stage production called *Sonia*.

A very active literary world has also evolved among the Latvians who fled Latvia at the time of the Soviet takeover and settled in various parts of the Western world. Some of the famous names include the essayist and novelist Zenta Mauriņa, who settled in Germany and later became well known there among the Latvians. Moreover, a whole new generation of Latvian poets also developed in exile in New York and are referred to as the "Hell's Kitchen" school of poets.

The poet Andrejs Eglitis lived in Sweden during the decades after World War II, returning to live in Latvia shortly before his death. He is well known for his patriotic poetry, which describes the longings for the freedom of Latvia. His poem "God, Thy Earth Is Aflame" has been set to music and is considered an important reflection on Latvia's struggle for survival and freedom.

MUSIC

Music has long been a part of Latvian cultural life in both formal settings, such as opera houses and theaters, and informal ones, such as the family home or

The most popular Baltic folk instrument is the *kokle* (KO-kle), a stringed instrument dating back to the 13th century.

local inn. The enormous variety of musical styles reflects the influences on Latvia's culture from other countries. Latvian folk songs, or *dainas*, make up the largest and most important part of the musical culture of the country. Although 400,000 published dainas exist, there are more than a million dainas that have never been published or recorded formally. These songs are sung at special occasions, such as weddings, birthdays, and festivals, accompanied by traditional instruments. In the middle of the 19th century Latvia experienced a national cultural awakening. Noted composers of that era included Andrejs Jurjāns and Jāzeps Vītols. The Latvian Symphony Orchestra, founded in 1926, is internationally renowned, as is Kremerata Baltica, a string ensemble led by violinist Gidon Kremer.

OPERA AND BALLET

The Latvian National Opera, renamed the Opera and Ballet Theater under Soviet rule, was opened in 1919 and became a representative art institution

The Kamer Choir performing at the Latvian National Opera.

of the country. It received substantial government support, which allowed it to keep admission fees low and attract many ordinary people to attend. Visits to the opera remained a popular activity for Latvians, particularly during times of oppression and unrest under Soviet and German rule.

The activities of the opera company included opera performances, symphonic concerts, and solo concerts by leading musicians. The National Opera also played an important role in promoting the works of Latvian composers. A number of Latvian operas were composed and performed between 1920 and 1940. Even during the Soviet occupation, the National Opera continued to perform classical Russian and standard Western repertoire.

Since independence in 1991, the National Opera building has received a major facelift, restoring the original facilities to their former grandeur and adding new ones. Latvian National Opera performances continue to attract major guest performers from Europe and elsewhere, and opening nights are

After Soviet leader Joseph Stalin's death in 1953, there was a period of revival of pre-Soviet Latvian culture. Some Latvian writers and composers, who had been deported to Siberia, were allowed to return to Latvia and work again.

The exterior of the National Opera House.

gala social events. The ballet company of the National Opera began its work in 1919, with the first performance taking place in 1922. From 1922 to 1944, the National Opera ballet produced 28 one-acts and 23 longer ballets, with a total number of 1,536 performances. Soloists performed as guest artists in Europe and elsewhere, and the whole company appeared in guest performances in Sweden and Poland. The Latvian State Ballet opened in 1932. Among its students were Alexander Godunov, and Mikhail Baryshnikov, who was born in Riga, Latvia, to Russian parents. In 1974 he defected to the West while on a performance tour in Canada.

THEATER

Professional theater also emerged in Latvia during the National Awakening in the second half of the 19th century with the production of the first play in Latvian, written by Ādolfs Alunāns, the founder of Latvian drama. The first performance took place in Riga in 1868. Latvian professional theater dates from 1886, when the Latvian Society in Riga provided space and funding to support professional actors, laying the foundation for the National Theater of Latvia in Riga, which continues to be one of the foremost theaters in Latvia to this day.

A second theater was founded in Latvia in 1902—*Jaunais Rigas Teatris* (New Rega Theater)—and the reputation of this theater was established with the production of the historical-symbolical plays by Jānis Rainis. The set designs were by Jānis Kuga, whose scenery and costumes enjoyed wide popularity.

The Daile Theater, founded in 1920, has a capacity of 1,000 seats, making it the largest theater in Latvia. It offers regular production of modern foreign plays in addition to traditional Latvian dramas.

FOLK SONGS

Music as a cultural expression most accurately represents the Latvian character, as it has been very important in the formation and maintenance of national feelings over the centuries. Folk songs are by far the most original and extensive part of Latvian musical tradition.

Latvian folk songs have been passed on from ancient times by direct and verbal communication from one generation to the next. They began to be collected in written form in the 19th century, and this continues to the present day.

The famous Latvian folklorist Krišjānis Barons spent 37 years classifying the texts of *dainas*, collecting more than 218,000 songs, of which about 35,800 were original. The total number of collected songs is now so vast that they outnumber the population of the country by two to one!

Latvian folk melodies have influenced the compositions of many Latvian composers of classical music. Pauls Dambis is known for his arrangements of Latvian folk melodies, and Imants Kalniņš and Raimonds Pauls are well-known composers. The most famous and prolific Latvian musician is the conductor Mariss Jansons, who conducts many of Europe's best-known orchestras.

Latvians singing folk songs during the Ligo Diena (Grass Day) Festival.

DAINAS

The dominant subject of Latvian folk songs is the material and spiritual life of the people. The words deal with the cycle of human life, from cradle to grave, and the songs are arranged this way in the published collections. The first volume contains cradle songs, the second volume love songs, while the third volume has songs about marriage and married life. The fourth volume is on work and everyday life.

A *daina* can be philosophical, humorous, joyful, sarcastic, gentle, instructive, comic, or witty, but actually has very little direct connection with history. Proper names are used to refer only to mythological characters and to those found in the ancient religions. Most *dainas* are composed of four-line verses that are divided into two—the first two lines ask a question, and the last two give the answer.

Traditional instruments are still used in folk music performances.

SONGS FOR CELEBRATION

Melodies for these songs can be either recitative in style—sung in a group with a lead singer and a responding choir—or solo songs, which are sung solo or in a group. Recitative songs do not have a regular text, as the words are improvised according to the requirements of the subject matter and conditions under which the singing takes place. They are sung to mark the celebration of the seasons or the major events of life—birth, christening, marriage, funerals—or as work songs telling about plowing, threshing, or herding. The solo song texts deal with romance, the beauty of nature, or the sorrows of children and orphans.

FOLK SONG FESTIVALS

Folk song festivals have become an important part of the Latvian culture. The first nationwide Latvian Song Festival took place in 1873 in Riga to foster and advance choral singing. The choir consisted of several thousand singers (the audience totaled four or five times that number), whereas at the ninth festival in 1938 the chorus consisted of 17,000 singers! From the very first song festival the tradition developed that a nationwide song festival would be held at intervals of four to eight years as an important demonstration of Latvian culture and national unity. In July 2008 the 24th Song Festival took place in Riga.

LATVIAN SONG FESTIVAL

The program for the Latvian Song Festival has become quite extensive. In addition to the concerts, programs now include arts and crafts exhibitions, folk dance performances, theater, and all kinds of instrumental, vocal, and religious concerts.

The festival may last four to five days or more, and although the main festival takes place in Riga, regional concerts and performances are held throughout Latvia in the weeks before the festival. For the past 50 years similar song festivals have also been held in many other cities around the world where Latvians have taken refuge.

A man making traditional toys and trinkets during a cultural exhibition.

TRADITIONAL ARTS AND CRAFTS

Latvia has retained a distinctive folk art, which has its roots in the ancient past but continues to be active and vibrant to this day. Over the centuries traditional art was evident in buildings and furniture, as well as in the clothes and jewelry that were created for the everyday needs of the rural population. Traditionally many peasants mastered several crafts and produced their own tools, utensils, and simple pieces of furniture. In addition, each parish had its own craftsmen who specialized in a particular trade.

The fundamental character of Latvian ornamental design is geometric and abstract, and these traditional designs are still applied to contemporary decorative and applied arts, most commonly in ceramics, metalwork, woodwork, textiles, and wickerwork. The creation of applied decorative arts continues to be a dominant and widespread activity in today's cultural life in Latvia.

Fine arts in Latvia found expression from the late 19th century. The best-known Latvian painters of that period were Jānis Rozentāls (1866—1916) and Vilhelms Purvītis (1872—1945).

Latvians love to sing. It is unusual to find a Latvian who has not sung in a choir or some group at some point in his or her life. For this reason Latvia is called "the singing nation." Folk songs are one of Latvia's national treasures and date back over a thousand years. The Latvian folk song or *daina* is a form of oral art that has the elements of tradition, literature, and symbolism. More than 1.2 million texts and 30,000 melodies have been identified.

LEISURE

Latvian youths playing on the City Council Square.

WITH INCREASING ECONOMIC stability in Latvia, activities that require expensive sports equipment, such as skiing and sailing, are gaining in popularity, and people are devoting more leisure time to reading and attending cultural events such as concerts, theater, opera, and other performing arts.

Latvians also love to stroll through their city or town parks, taking evening or Sunday afternoon walks, enjoying some gentle exercise with

Children can play in the myraid parks and playgrounds scattered throughout Latvia's towns.

Latvians are able to spend more time and money on leisure activities with the country's increasing stability. They are now able to participate in activities such as sailing and attending concerts and various arts events. Latvians also enjoy being outdoors and playing traditional games. Other popular activities include singing, swimming, and winter sports.

105

the whole family. Hunting and fishing, hiking, gardening, traditional folk dancing and singing, and craft-making are also popular leisure activities.

Games are an integral part of the traditional culture of Latvians. Generally there are two types—games with music, where the players sing along during the game, and games without music, where participants must perform certain actions.

TRADITIONAL GAMES

A traditional game that may be played by children is called *Viens*, *divi*, *trīs*, *pēdējais pāris šķiras!* (One, two, three, last couple separate!). Participants form a column, in pairs, except for a single person at the front of the column

Chess is a popular pasttime for Latvians.

Some young people like learning traditional lace-making.

who does not have a partner. He/she calls out: "*pēdējais pā ris šķiras!*" On hearing this, the last couple in the column runs to the front of the column, while the single player tries to catch one of them before they reach the front of the line. Whoever remains single takes over the shouting until a partner is caught again.

Another popular game that is still played in the countryside, takes place during Easter. A swing is constructed and hung in the farmyard or nearby woods, and all the inhabitants take a turn on the swing on Easter morning. Gifts are exchanged—particularly colorful Easter eggs—and unmarried men receive hand-knitted mittens or colorful woven sashes from unmarried women, as a token of love.

STORYTELLING

Despite centuries of foreign dominance, it was through the oral tradition that Latvians developed their culture and identity and preserved their sense of nationality.

The most popular activity is singing, but folktales and legends, anecdotes, riddles, proverbs, folk beliefs, and sayings are common, too. The usual subject matter is everyday rural life and social customs and behavior.

RIDDLES

Some 450,000 riddles have been collected by the Latvian Folklore Institute. They are short, usually only two to six words long, and are expressed simply and succinctly. Most have only one correct answer. For example, "What always wears a green frock, summer and winter?" is a spruce tree; "What does not have hands, does not have a loom, yet weaves?" is a spider; "What is high above during the day, down below during the night?" is the sun; and "What flies like a bird but is not a bird, stings like a snake but is not a snake?" is a mosquito. Folk sayings and parables represent collective folk wisdom. Many of the sayings are common to those of other European cultures because they came into Latvia through the church.

A NEW FREEDOM

Since the return to independence in Latvia, people have enjoyed a freedom they had not experienced before. The younger generations had never had contact with cultures of the West before the end of Soviet rule. Today, through the popularity of American and European music, movies, and books, leisure activities that were once restricted have broadened. The older generations are relishing a return to their national identity, and apart from spending time discussing the fascinating historical changes they have experienced, many prefer to catch up with old friends over a game of chess or cards.

SPORTS

Sports are popular in Latvia. Soccer, basketball, volleyball, track and field, wrestling, tennis, ice hockey, orienteering, motor sports, or even beach volleyball all take place, weather permitting, around the country.

Swimming is popular with Latvian youngsters, and there are municipal pools in most big towns and cities. Schools also encourage swimming as part of the physical education curriculum. Latvians also are known for winter sports such as bobsled and hockey. They are usually placed in the top eight for both sports at the Olympics.

Latvia's debut in the Olympics took place in 1924 when 38 athletes joined in the summer games. The most famous early Olympian was the long-distance walker, Jānis Dalins, who won the silver medal for the 31-mile (50-km) walk in 1932. In total, since the 1952 Olympic Games, Latvian athletes have won 20 gold, 32 silver, and 16 bronze medals, including those they won while competing as part of the Soviet Union between 1952 and 1988. In the 1992 Winter Olympics, Latvia rejoined the Olympic organization as an independent nation. Igors Vihrovs won a gold medal in gymnastics in 2004, and Māris Strombergs won a gold medal in BMX bicycle racing in 2008.

Latvia's Rihards Veide (number 251) at a practice run of the BMX Supercross 2009 competition.

FESTIVALS

A Latvian woman dressed in a traditional costume at the midsummer festival in Jurmala.

CHAPTER 12

LATVIA HAS MANY DIFFERENT festivals that celebrate secular and religious traditions and major historical events.

Latvian festivals tend to be seasonal. The festival of Mārtiņi takes place at the beginning of November, when the religious festivities begin for Christmas and last until after the New Year. There are various festivities in the springtime, celebrating the equinox and the beginning of the summer. The biggest festival of the year, Jāņi Diena, celebrates the summer solstice and involves singing, dancing, and feasting. Houses are cleaned and foliage is used to make wreaths and garlands.

Traditionally, at the end of the summer, there are two more festivals—one in August to celebrate the end of the hot period and

Young children dressed for the biggest Latvian festival of the year, Jāņi Diena.

Due to Latvia's unique history, many festivals celebrated are a combination of ancient and contemporary beliefs. Common features in many festivals are singing and dancing. Christian holidays such as Christmas and Easter are also celebrated and are usually family affairs. Historical holidays commemorating the struggle for independence are also observed.

another in September to welcome the fall equinox and remember the souls of the dead.

MIDSUMMER MADNESS

Many of the festivals combine ancient beliefs with modern celebration, and nowhere is this more apparent than in Latvia's most popular holiday, Jāņi Diena (Jani's Day). The festival, which celebrates midsummer, begins on the evening of June 23 and continues into the next day. As the festival approaches, songs with a special refrain resound everywhere, awaiting the arrival of Jānis (pronounced Yah-niss), the son of God, who personifies the festival. Generally, Jānis is pictured as a tall and handsome man, dressed in beautiful

Enormous bunches of foliage are gathered to create the wreaths and headdresses that are worn during Jāņi Diena.

clothes and riding a large horse. He wears the traditional adornment of the occasion—a wreath of oak leaves—on his head.

On the evening of June 23, called Līgo Vakars or Jāņi Vakars (Jani's Eve), the celebration of the summer solstice takes place. Jani's Eve has retained most of its ancient pre-Christian flavor. This means a whole night of singing, dancing, merriment, and fortune-telling, until the sun comes up the next morning. Special beer is brewed, and a special cheese is prepared. After dusk, fires are lit on the hilltops.

WREATHS AND DECORATIONS

June 23 is also considered the best day of the year to gather medicinal herbs. Flowers and greenery are collected to make wreaths of flowers for the women

Many festivals are also a time when family and friends can gather over a feast.

and men—especially men named Jānis (the most common men's name)—to wear during the festivities. Everything is decorated with greenery, while mountain ash branches, thistles, and other sharp objects are placed over building entrances to ward off evil spirits.

The following day's activities include old customs believed to enlist the aid of the spirits of the home, field, and forest. They are intended to help provide a good harvest, by shielding crops and livestock from evil.

CHRISTIAN HOLIDAYS

Many Latvian holidays are very similar to those in other Western countries. Latvians celebrate all the main holidays of the Christian world, with the biggest celebrations taking place at Easter and Christmas.

Latvians love to dress up, and their many festivals give them the opportunity to create wild and wonderful costumes.

There are echoes in the modern celebrations of ancient festivals that were once observed in Latvia at the same time of year before the coming of Christianity. Christmas and Easter are times for reflection and jubilation for both Christian and non-Christian families. They are special occasions when the whole family can gather together. Latvians always celebrate in style, and everyone makes an effort to dress up for the occasion.

CHRISTMAS

Christmas—the Latvian word for the holiday is Ziemassvētki, meaning "winter feast"—celebrates not only the birth of Jesus Christ, but also reflects a direct connection with the ancient winter solstice celebrations held by Latvians long ago.

Christmas is by far the most festive occasion for Latvians—the return of light at the winter solstice is heralded by the arrival of the celestial beings

A young Latvian child visits Santa's grotto in a Riga department store.

called Dievadeli and the Four Brothers Ziemassvētki, who represent the four days traditionally allowed for celebration of the Christmas period.

Typically at this time, houses are decorated with decorations of straw and feather, and with *puzuri* (PU-zu-ri), diamond-shaped chandelier decorations made from straw or twigs. Tables are set high with generous amounts of different foods, such as pig's snout, bacon rolls, and boiled brown peas.

THE *BUDUĻU* CUSTOM

During the weeks before Christmas, the *buduļu* custom is celebrated. Disguised in costumes and accompanied by singing, dancing, and much joviality, people call on their friends and neighbors. The festive masqueraders represent good

The sieve man, on the left, is a symbol of fertility, appearing prior to Christmas as part of the *buduļu* (BU-du-lu) custom.

spirits, whose songs and dances are intended to bring good luck to people and fertility to the fields and livestock. Their dances are characterized by "stomping" steps designed to stomp out all the weeds from the fields. The procession also drags a Yule log along, to be burned at the last stop. This represents the sun recovering its warmth, as well as consuming the past year's misfortunes.

FESTIVAL ACTIVITIES

Fortune-telling is a popular activity during Christmas and New Year celebrations. Molten lead is poured into water where it solidifies into an

Schoolchildren collect colorful spring flowers in preparation for Easter festivities.

Many festivals were celebrated in Latvia years ago, marking the changing seasons. Ritual activities took place and special foods were eaten.

Meteņi (February 18—19)

Celebrated the end of ķekatas (TYEH-kah-tuss)—the carnival activities of Christmas—with sleigh rides and masquerades. Weavers made cloth with their freshly spun yarns, and on the farm young horses were broken in.

Great Day (March 21)

Celebrated on the day and night of equal length—the spring equinox. The ritual activities included washing before sunrise in running water, hanging swings, and chasing birds. It was the time when the days were longer, and the farmers no longer had to use lights in the evenings.

Jani's Day, or Jāņi Diena, is one of the oldest Latvian holidays and is a well-known festival throughout Eastern Europe. Beer is brewed especially for the day, and a cheese called Janu Cheese is made using caraway seeds.

abstract form. The future is predicted by studying the shape of the shadow cast on a wall by this "sculpture."

Similarly a common tradition on Easter Sunday in Latvia is for neighbors to gather at a swing hung from a pole between two trees and watch as young people try to swing as high as the treetops. Swinging high ensures a good harvest during the coming summer. Gifts are also exchanged, particularly colorful Easter eggs.

HISTORICAL HOLIDAYS

Some of the Latvian holidays also celebrate events that have made deep impressions on Latvia's history and on the lives of its people.

June 14 is the commemoration day of victims of the communist terror when, on the night of June 13, 1941, the first mass deportations were made

Ūsiņi *(April 19–20)*

The official beginning of summer, celebrated many centuries ago, when roosters were killed in order to silence them, and their blood was drained into horse troughs. Crosses were painted on doors with the blood, and horses were taken to swim before sunrise. The ritual foods were eggs, boiled rooster, and beer. The evening grazing of horses and cattle began, and it was plowing and sowing time for the farmers.

Jāņi Diena *(June 23–24)*

The longest day and shortest night—the summer solstice. The activities were similar to those of today—flower wreaths were made, bonfires were lit, and songs were sung. The ritual foods were cheese, bread, pies, meat dishes, and beer. On the farm, haying started.

Apjumības *or* **Rudenāji** *(September 23)*

The fall equinox and the beginning of the period of the shadows, when the spirits of the dead visit. Lots of meat was eaten and winter crops were sown.

Mārtiņi *(November 10)*

The end of the celebration of the souls and the beginning of masquerade time, leading up to Christmas. Mārtiņi balls—made of peas, beans, potatoes, and hemp— were the festival food.

by the Soviet powers. Some 15,000 Latvians from all walks of life, including the old, the sick, children, and even babies, were arrested without trial, and without legal justification, were herded into freight trains and transported under guard to Siberia to forced labor camps or gulags.

November 11, Lacplesis's Day, is the memorial day of the fight for independence, commemorating all who have fought in defense of Latvia. November 18 celebrates Latvia's declaration of independence in 1918, and May 4 is the date of the declaration of renewed independence in 1990.

FOOD

A fruit and vegetable stand at Central Market in Riga.

I N ANCIENT LATVIA FOOD WAS traditionally prepared in one of two main locations—the house where everyone lived or in a specially constructed building with an open hearth.

In the latter case the hearth was usually placed as far away from the other farm buildings as possible. Most dishes were cooked in a cast-iron pot, placed on an open fire. Water was carried up from the well and stored in wooden pails.

Basic food staples were homegrown, preserved, and prepared. The basic foods were grains, various kinds of meat, saltwater fish

Wild strawberries for sale at the market.

As in most Western countries, Latvians consume about three meals a day. Bread is an important staple to the Latvian diet and usually accompanies every meal. Latvian food is traditionally bland, due to an absence of strong spices used. Dairy products are also popular among Latvians, as are fruits during the summer.

Depending on the season, a wide variety of fruits can be found for sale in the market.

(or preserved fish in some regions), and dairy products. Commonly grown garden vegetables such as potatoes, cabbage, beets, turnips, carrots, peas, and beans were also eaten, as were wild greens—sorrel, nettles, thistle, and goosefoot—in the spring and wild berries such as strawberries, bilberries, raspberries, loganberries, wild hazelnuts, and mushrooms in the late summer and fall.

BREAD

Bread was—and still is—a staple food at every meal, baked from rye or barley flour, or for special occasions, from wheat or buckwheat flour. Dough for bread was prepared in a large, elongated wooden trough, approximately 4 feet (1.2 m) in length, with handles. The bread was baked in special ovens, where the loaf was placed on a flat, wide wooden shovel to be transferred onto the hot coals.

Baking was done in large quantities, usually in big loaves. On special occasions, rolls might also be baked, with butter and/or egg wash added, or with special toppings, such as grated carrots.

PORRIDGE AND MEAT

Years ago porridge was the most commonly served dish and was prepared from pearl barley and other grains. Vegetables, as well as milk, and some meat or lard were added. The content of the porridge or gruel usually depended on what produce was available at a given time of year, or the financial situation of the household.

Meat was consumed sparingly and on special occasions, since most of it was taken to the market to be sold. Only affluent families could afford

Workers preparing meat for sausage-making at a factory in Leipaja.

Fresh fruit and vegetables, as well as a large variety of meat, are available in Latvia.

to eat meat regularly, and in the countryside fresh meat was often only available when an animal was slaughtered, usually in the fall. Every part of the animal was prepared for consumption—the best cuts were usually sold and the secondary cuts prepared for home consumption, including the blood, head, feet, and innards. Latvian meat dishes may include fowl, beef, horse meat, pork, and fish. Families who lived along the coasts smoked fishlike eel, flounder, lamprey, and cod.

EXTRA FLAVORS

Latvian food is traditionally bland and without strong spices. Caraway seeds, onions, and garlic improve the taste. Ground hemp seed prepared with salt and green onions is sometimes used in place of butter. Fresh milk is added to porridge and gruel, or made into yogurt and cottage cheese. Latvians like to eat honey as a natural sweetener. Honey production is the business of many farms today.

DRINKS

Juice prepared from birch or maple sap was a very popular nonalcoholic drink. It was prepared in the springtime in large quantities so that it could last most of the summer.

Today ale and beer are sometimes home-brewed from barley with hops added and served at all important occasions, such as harvesting. It is sometimes available at pubs, along with commercially brewed drinks.

Latvians drinking wine at a festival.

MEALS

Latvians usually eat three meals a day. In the olden days, a fourth meal was often added in the afternoon. In those days, the midday meal was usually the main meal of the day—gruel served with lard or fat, and cabbage or sauerkraut. The afternoon extra meal included bread, cottage cheese, buttermilk, and sometimes herring. Latvians have always been great fans of dairy products. Milk, *rūgušpiens* (a sour, carbonated drink, similar to yogurt, with a little bit of alcohol), cottage cheese, cream, cheese, and butter are eaten at almost every meal. For supper Latvians ate potatoes with a flour or

A Latvian family having a meal together.

mushroom gravy, or milk gruel with bread. Each day of the week a particular type of dish was served, and supper on Saturdays as well as the meals on Sundays might also include some special dishes or treats.

EAT, DRINK, AND BE MERRY

Latvians are known for their strong hospitality. Regardless of the economic situation of the host, a guest will be treated to all that the host has. Often the poorest people are the most hospitable, and nothing is spared. Latvians like to entertain, and a formal dinner is taken seriously. Like other inhabitants of the northern countries, Latvians like to eat and drink, but they do not drink more than any other European and they usually have drinks together with a meal.

Homemade beer is popular in Latvia and is a great topic of conversation at dinner parties.

Skaba putra—consisting of cooked barley oats with buttermilk, yogurt, or milk—and *miestins*—dry pieces of rye bread soaked in water and honey—were popular snacks for hungry Latvian farmers in the early 1900s.

Dishes prepared for a Latvian feast are chosen according to the produce available at a particular time of year, but the central dish of any festive meal is the meat course. Food is most plentiful in the fall when the harvest has been brought in—special breads are baked for the occasion. Oven-baked turnips are served and also carrots, peas, potatoes (cooked and served with fried smoked bacon), onions, and hemp seed, formed into balls. Honey and apples are served for dessert, as well as a rich cake on very special occasions.

FALL FEASTS

Traditionally, special family occasions were usually held in the fall when food was plentiful, and on special feast days such as Mārtiņi (November 10), goose or capon was served. For Christmas and New Year's Eve, traditional dishes included smoked pig's snout, braised sauerkraut or cabbage, and blood pudding served with red bilberry preserves, peas, and beans. For special occasions in the spring, eggs were the favorite dish, as well as jellied veal or pork and milk pudding. For summer festivities, the traditional dishes were made with dairy products, such as cheeses, served with specially baked rolls,

A family enjoying a picnic.

butter, and *piragi* (PEE-raa-gi)—crescent-shaped baked buns filled with savory onion and bacon.

LATVIAN FOOD TODAY

Latvian cuisine has been influenced by German, Swedish, and Russian cuisine. Today the foods that Latvians eat are very similar to those eaten in many other countries. Breakfast usually consists of coffee, boiled or fried eggs, fried potatoes, rye or white bread, and butter or cottage cheese.

Lunch may be a hearty soup with meat, and a meat dish followed by a dessert of fruit compote, bread pudding, or a bread soup with raisins or apples.

A Latvian supper may consist of many different dishes, such as milk soup, pasta, porridge with meat, fried fish, boiled potatoes with pork, or cottage cheese. After supper, the typical Latvian may drink milk, tea, or coffee with bread, butter, jam, or honey.

On Sundays there is usually a more elaborate meal with a special main course, such as meat patties, meat loaf, or cabbage rolls, and desserts such as pancakes with jam or a fruit fool are prepared.

These impressive cakes are typical examples of Latvian treats made at Christmastime.

FISH IN MILK WITH BOILED POTATOES

1¼ lb. (560 g) mackerel, perch or pilchards

5 oz (140 g) mix of onion, parsley, and carrots

1½ cups (375 ml) hot milk

2 tablespoons (30 ml) vegetable oil

2 tablespoons (30 ml) sour cream

Chopped parsley or dill

Pinch of salt

Dash of pepper

1 bay leaf

3 small potatoes, boiled and skinned

Cut fish into pieces or cutlets. Slice onions into rings. Coarsely grate carrots, and chop parsley. Arrange fish cutlets with vegetables in a saucepan. Add vegetable oil, salt, and pepper. Pour over hot milk, add bay leaf and simmer over low heat for 10 to 15 minutes. Add sour cream at the end of cooking. Serve fish with the cooking liquid and boiled potatoes. Sprinkle with chopped herbs before serving.

DEBESSMANNA (WHIPPED CRANBERRY WITH MILK)

3 oz (85 g) fresh cranberries (or other berries)

1 cup (250 ml) water

½ cup (115 g) sugar

¼ cup (62 g) semolina

Rinse cranberries. Reserve a few pieces for garnishing. Crush the rest of the cranberries and squeeze out juice into a bowl. Place cranberry pulp in a saucepan, cover with water, and boil for 5 minutes over medium heat. Remove the pulp with a strainer. Add sugar into the liquid. Gradually add the semolina, stirring constantly with a wooden spoon until semolina thickens. Add reserved cranberry juice, and stir until well mixed. Pour mixture into a bowl and cool rapidly. Whip mixture until it becomes light and airy and has doubled or tripled in volume. Serve in deep dessert dishes with cold milk. Place a piece of cranberry in each dish.

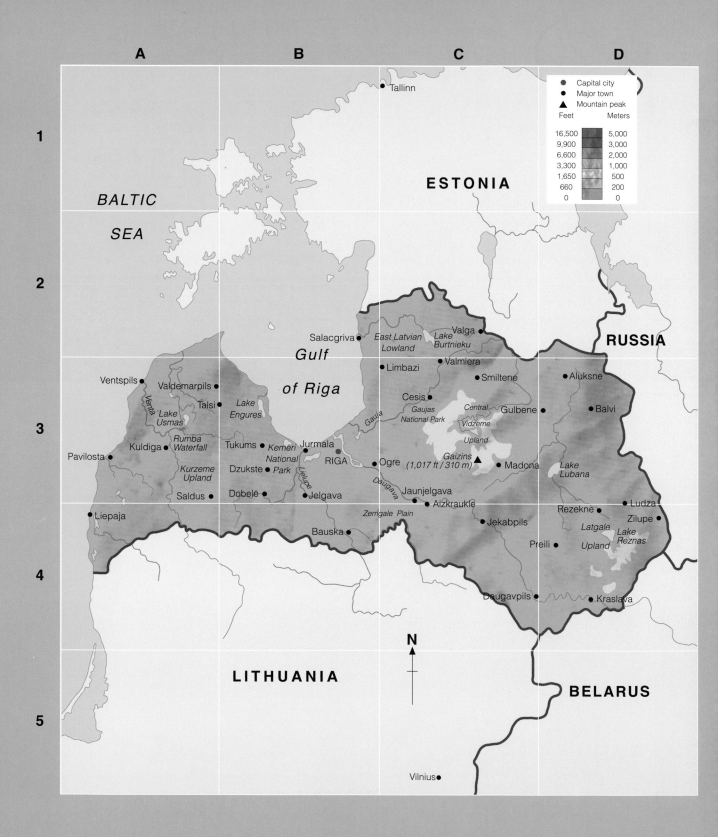